T0160826

SCENES OF LIFE AT THE CAPITAL

Scenes of Life at the Capital

PHILIP WHALEN

of

Life

EDITED AND WITH AN
AFTERWORD BY DAVID BRAZIL

WAVE BOOKS

at

SEATTLE AND NEW YORK

the

Capital

Published by Wave Books

www.wavepoetry.com

Copyright © 2020 by The Estate of Philip Whalen

Afterword copyright © 2020 by David Brazil

All rights reserved

Wave Books titles are distributed to the trade by

Consortium Book Sales and Distribution

Phone: 800-283-3572 / SAN 631-760X

Library of Congress Cataloging-in-Publication Data

Names: Whalen, Philip, author. | Brazil, David (Poet), author of afterword.

Title: Scenes of life at the capital / Philip Whalen ; afterword by David Brazil.

Description: Seattle : Wave Books, [2020]

Identifiers: LCCN 2019030141 | ISBN 9781940696928 (trade paperback)

Classification: LCC PS3545.H117 S3 2020 | DDC 811/.54—dc23

LC record available at https://lccn.loc.gov/2019030141

Designed by Crisis

Printed in the United States of America

Scenes of Life at the Capital was originally published
by Grey Fox Press, Bolinas, CA, 1971, and reprinted in
The Collected Poems of Philip Whalen (Wesleyan University
Press, 2007). Reprinted with permission of The Estate
of Philip Whalen and Wesleyan University Press. Scans
from Philip Whalen's notebooks appear courtesy of
The Bancroft Library, University of California, Berkeley.

9 8 7 6 5 4 3 2 1

Scenes of Life at the Capital

of

Life

FOR

ALLEN GINSBERG

at

the

Capital

Having returned at last and being carefully seated
On the floor—somebody else's floor, as usual—
Far away across that ocean which looked
Through Newport windows years ago—somebody else's livingroom—
Another messed-up weedy garden
Tall floppy improbably red flowers
All the leaves turned over in the rain
Ridged furry scrotum veins

Hedges glisten tile roof tin roof telephone pole
Decoratively tormented black pine
Slowly repeating its careful program
Endlessly regretting but here is original done once
Not to be reproduced nor electronically remembered

Loosten up.   Festoon.

An enormous drop of pure water suddenly there
Right in the center of preceding page

Nothing can be done about that. The line was ruined. OK.
Belt hair. A bend is funnier. Bar Kochba. Do something
About it. Like animal factory mayhem.

The master said, "You shouldn't have put
Yourself into such a position
In the first place." Nevertheless,
It all looks different, right to left.
Another master said, "Well,
You can always take more, you know."

The wind went by just now
South Dakota. Who's responsible for this
Absurd revival of the Byzantine Empire,
Sioux Falls-Mitchell-Yankton area?
Further anomalies of this order will receive
Such punishment as a Court Martial may direct
Or the discretion of the Company Commander
Failure to conform with these regulations
Shall be punished by Court Martial
TAKE ALL YOU WANT BUT EAT ALL YOU TAKE
The following named Enlisted Men are transf
R E S T R I C T E D. SPECIAL ORDER #21 this
HQ dd 8 Feb 1946 contained 6 Pars. C E N S O R E D
3. Fol EM, White, MCO indicated, ASRS indicated,
AF2AF, are reld fr asgmt and dy this HQ and trfd
in gr to 37th AAFBU, Dorje Field, Lhasa, TIBET
and WP at such time as will enable them to arrive thereat
not later than 20 Feb 1946 rptg to CO for dy C E N S O R E D
Or such punishment as a Court Martial may direct
I used to travel that way.

Always take a little more. This is called
"A controlled habit." (Don't look at me,
I never said a murmuring word.)
Didn't you say, "polished water"?
I normally wouldn't say so.

Wasp in the bookshelf rejects Walt Whitman,
Herman Melville, Emily Dickinson, The Goliard Poets,
A Vedic Reader, Lama Govinda, Medieval French Verses & Romances,
Long Discourses of the Buddha, and The Principal Upanishads.
Window glass reads more entertainingly
But soon that too is left for the foxtail grass
Camellia hedge, the dull mid-morning sun

followed by accidental descent into goofball drift
unintentionally
but such is the cost of knowledge
recollections of Jack in Berkeley
Nembies & grass & wine
Geraniums, ripe apricots, & plums
Clio's green and slanting eyes
Gentle smile of pointed face
How much love I owe to her and to all women

My mother tried to warn me,
"Let your sister ride the bike a while;
Don't be so damned selfish!"

How can Victorian American lady
Explain to her son that his cock
Doesn't belong exclusively to himself
But also to certain future women?

It's a matter of some reassurance
That we are physically indistinguishable from other men.
When introspection shows us
That we have different degrees of intelligence
Varying capacities for knowing morality
We lose something of our complacency

Rooty-toot
Rooty-toot
We're the boys
From the Institute
I wondered recently what school was being lampooned
In this impudent snatch of gradeschool melody
Recollection of obscene & early childhood.
If Socrates and Plato and Diotima
And all the rest of the folks at that party
Had simply eaten lots of food and wine and dope
And spent the entire weekend in bed together
Perhaps Western Civilization
Wouldn't have been such a failure?

Rooty-toot, Plato's Original Institute

Much of the morning sweeping consists of clearing away
Bodies of several hundred insects who followed my lightglobes
And perished here.
After 49 days each one of them will be reborn
Each in a different shape in a different world
Each according to the quality of his actions
In all his past existences. What a system.
Hi-de-ho.

Rooty-toot-toot. Normally I wouldn't say no.
Rooty-toot is what any bugle, horn or trumpet
Is thought of as "saying," the sound of a fart.
Years later I found the trumpeting devils in the *Inferno*

MUSH

All dropped untidy into the bottom of my skull
A warped red plastic phonograph record (the label says
Emperor Concerto) floats on top, inaudible;
Nevertheless, light comes through it in a pleasant way
Precisely the color of raspberry licorice whips.
It got bent in the mail, too near the steampipes . . .
The music is in there someplace, squeezed into plastic
At enormous expense of knowledge,

"FIRE IN THE BORGO"

luke-warm mush, then cold milk poured over it
chills and transforms the entire arrangement gradually
tending towards an ineradicable (nonbiodegradable)
plastic resembling "Bakelite," shiny brown
It shatters if you drop it hard

Changed again! Turned 180 degrees in an
Unexpected direction
Bent Beethoven, *Burnt Njal* I have lived
All these years until this moment
Without understanding there's absolutely nothing
Which I can do well
                    (RING BELL THREE TIMES)

            N O T H I N G
"Har-de-har."
What do you mean, "Har-de-har"?
Nothing, just "Har-de-har."
I might have said, "Hi-de-ho."

"O Mighty Nothing!"   (How does the Wicked Earl begin?)

        "Then all proceeded from the great united . . ." (what?)

        "And from thy fruitful emptiness's hand
        Snatch'd Men, Beasts, Birds, Fire, (Water), Air and Land"

John Wilmot Earl of Rochester.
The parenthesized water is presented to us
On good authority by the Editor, Vivian De Sola Pinto.
I found my mother's name
Written there three hundred years ago.

"I don't know whether we can or not. Hee-hee! Let's try!"

WALK   LIGHT!

I don't know nothing about it
There are two long-bearded apprehensive gremlins
One beside each of my ears. The left-hand one
Very gently whispers, "Hello?" and
Listens for a reply from the other side.
He repeats, "Hello?" very softly. "Are you
Still there?" And the right-hand one listening
And nodding, his own ear turned towards that furry dark
Pink and lavender cave. Presently he replies
(Also very softly) "Hello!"
Across the blank echoing empty dark between.

I think I'll go take a bath.
Well, come on, who is it, if it isn't gremlins—
Some other of those revolting British creations for children
Subject of PhD theses in American universities

Big eyes, charm, lots of fur all over
Stage-set by Arthur Rackham
I'm really going to take a bath now.
I split wood (gift of the landlord) while water
Plooshes into iron pot.
Make fire underneath.
Bless these elements! Their nature and use
Connect me to this place (The Capital) its history
Temple bell rings (No Self. No Permanence.)
Fiery waters all around
The iron bathtub is history, its name, *goemon-buro*
A Goemon bath, he was a highway robber, caught at last
And cooked to death in a pot of boiling oil
On the bank of the Kamo River.

Unveiling and Elevation of the Wienie

(RING GONG THREE TIMES)

Kyoto October 2, 1969 a graceful poem
In fond & grateful memory of Mr W. S. All Happinesse
Outline of Hieizan almost invisible behind the hedge
(Not my hedge but the one at Daitokuji Hojo)
Kamo River uniform white lines pouring down
Solidly moulded over stone barrage
Foam across great fitted paving blocks (The Dalles!)

Its man-made bed

        rowdy-dow

                beyond the foam thick purple

From dye-vats along Takano River

Green shaved patch on dark mountainside   DAIMONJI

which we saw as a pattern of fire from Arashiyama Bridge

paper lanterns floating in the River Oi

Souls returning to the flowery shore,

the Wind's Angelic Face

Puffing, happy Wallace Stevens Birthday

Heavenly Baroque paradise where he sails

Far New Haven's Other Shore

Cherubic winds flap his coronation robes

Dash silver on his golden harp and starry brow

An extravagant Handelian heaven

Lavender wings of peacock feather eyes

All Memling enamel (Mr Yeats a little jealous)

Harps of "omnipotent power"

        ("OHO, OMNIPOTENT POW-ER

        OHO! OH JOY DIVINE!"

        Gregory Corso imitating Peter Ustinov Nero–movie)

Too busy to see anybody in New York
A few French paintings, shoeshine
New tweed English pants two pounds real Camembert cheese
Who is there to see in New York anyway
Everybody's moved to Bolinas (I dreamed last night of Margot Doss)
And so home again, among roses "Arcades of Philadelphia
The Past" a piece of Idaho scenic agate
A crystal ball "Of Hartford in a Purple Light"
And supper on "An Ordinary Evening in New Haven"
Where you never lived but always heaven
Along with Stéphane Mallarmé and all the marble swans.

I keep thinking about all the really great ones
(To paraphrase Mr Spender) I think
Like anybody living in a foreign country
Of home and money . . . .
There's probably *Some* sensible human way of living in America
Without being rich or drunk or taking dope all the time

FRED, IS THAT MUSIC? DO I SHAKE OR WEEP?
3:X:69 Thomas Wolfe's Birthday "he'd say ok and we'd start in
and every time I'd presently find myself going involuntarily
ulk, ulk, ulk, which seemed to inspire him to even wilder
extravagances,"
FRED IS THAT *MUSIC?* DO I FAKE OR LEAP?

To my horror & chagrin I see that I've suppressed
Lots of goody in the process of copying from ms to typewriter;
Mike warned me years ago, "You should always
Make them reproduce your handwritten pages."
                    (OVERLAP)
overleaf clover
I said

                rowdy-dow
                (picture of leaves)

                                        poo.

beyond the foam
thick purple. Takano River dye-vats
there's not a way in the world I can explain that to you
you just have to get in and start doing it yourself
      green shaved patch
      right half of the big DAIMONJI

"Every place is the same
Because I felt the same, remembering everything
We boated for hours on the Lake of Constance
Went swimming in the Blue Grotto, ate sheep's eyes
And chicken guts in Crete. The blue tiles of Isfahan
Were better or worse than the blue tiles around the late
Mr ———, his swimming pool at San Simeon."
And the man from Intourist at Tbilisi who so much
Resembled him:
"Everything being the same everything is naturally different"

Here in the Shinshindo Coffee Shop again
that blonde young lady who just disappeared into—
and so swiftly reappeared out of—the *benjo* was not
that funny girl who used to write for *Newsweek* but may as well
have been—
right this minute
asleep in London, Sydney or Tashkent

three new little trees just beyond
north end of goldfish pond.
I peer among the branches
in search of the blonde who now sits inside
I am in arbor outside
the number of goldfish seven or nine
One is color of polished metal
that girl's hair is a paler shade

(streetcar fills the window 1½ seconds) the hard chairs
and benches here, big tables probably not like the ones
in Reed College library. Fits of psychic imperialism
I attach tags, carve initials, pee on fireplugs
outlining my territory
is that blonde still there
sort of ecru-colored minidress, thin cloth, heavy coat
thick pale hair, untidy braid half undone behind
small pointy nose, chin recedes a little
there's no point in returning until I find out

why did I have to come all the way back here
endless belt of punch-cards travels through the neighbor's loom
repetition of a pattern from a long time back

Here's one who eats a hardboiled egg, rolls, hot milk
and a picture magazine. His friend's weak eyes read
a little book
German metaphysics translated into literary Japanese
vague to vague
two giant galaxies passing through and beyond each
other, a radio receiver on a planet several thousand
light years off might well tune in
on a stupendous music,
  F O O O R E E E N G ! &c (Karl-Heinz Stockhausen)
chancre star
    when you get to the end,
      stop

Bill Whosis drunk & yelling in front of Sanjo Station
End of the Tokaido Road
Kamogawa sluicing fast under Sanjo Bridge
The wooden posts and railings shown by Hokusai
guard the asphalt concrete way
  "Why don't you walk?"

a way of living in America
doesn't really invite a narrow pen point plink

under they penthouse lid they eye they milky
forehead, Yaquina Bay, Yachats,
Neptune Park (Tillie the Whale flashes past
just north or south of Yachats?)

I can imagine living there as my grandmother did
gathering wild blackberries
driving out towards Gresham for a mess of green corn
time for melons, grapes & Chinook salmon
at The Dalles, dig mud clams at Netarts Bay
Family all over the place, friends from the old
Kilpatrick Hotel, bring blackberry jam
fresh string beans and salmon

She wanted her hotel in winter
good steam heat, parties and dances
The Lonesome Club, Cotillion Ballroom
Earliest spring flowers and pussywillows
Green slime and moss and mud evergreen and fern
smell of woman, beyond enormous plate-glass windows
The Studebaker black sedan.
All this lost again, galmed up for fair
where's the minute particulars?
what was I thinking of?

I keep thinking of those really great ones like Confucius:
"What am I supposed to do, become rich & famous?"

People keep introducing me to the famous English Poet
We have been introduced to each other once every ten years
For a very long time. He has no reason to remember meeting
Me, since the conversation is limited to "how do you do?"
And he's considerably taller than I am.

I think all the time I can't forgive him
For jamming that "nk" sound against the initial "C"
Nor for the blackmail word, "truly"
I can't stop thinking about . . .
I keep thinking all the time about those
Absolutely splendid
                    (that isn't so sharp, either)
Well, somewhere there's an exact & absolutely wild poetical
equivalent to Mr X's most often quoted line, & if he
had found it & used it
I should have swooned with awe & pleasure when I was first
introduced to him, & afterwards we might have been able
to talk together?

Fred, is that music?
Do I shake or weep? Did you fall or was you pushed?

Did I run and was I tired

Years gone by, twelve years agone
I must have had about me then some final faded blink of beauty

Fred asked me to marry him, he would be 21 fairly soon
I never had a greater compliment.
It's too bad we were sexually incompatible
He's the only one who ever asked me.
No matter how odd the fancy I remember him
Happily at the entrance to old age
I haven't been a total failure after all.

Paul Gauguin went someplace there was light enough to see
And it made him a painter. (?) N. Hawthorne to Italy
H. Melville to the Southern Sea, beyond the neighborhood of
Christian gentlefolk
Fred, is that music that I fake or leap?

Lion-faced Paul Gauguin fingers and toes
Cock and nose all sloughing gradually away
Leprosy melted him, northern snowman
Disadvantages of a lovely climate
"White men go to pieces in the Tropics"

I can't stop thinking about those who really knew
What they were doing, Paul Gauguin, John Wieners, LeRoi Jones
I keep thinking of those great ones who never fled the music
Fred and his roommate with bottled hair
All of them yarded off to Viet Nam
Translated into Rugged American Fighting Men
Defending the Free World against Godless Atheistic Communism

("I am a U.S. Marine.
I like to fuck and I like to fight:
What's it going to be?")

Which makes it impossible to like the *Iliad*
Sadist faggotry too much like Parris Island
The Green Berets and the cops back home
Somebody else's castration fantasies acted out

In an ideal climate
                but why should the world be different
                Why should it continue in its present
                nasty way? And it changes every
                nanosecond, lovely, dreadful, smashed
                dismembered and devoured by *prajna*
                Events like the Indo-China War
                Final quivers and tremblings
                Neural flashes in freshly killed men
                (movie of *Bonnie & Clyde*)
The longer I think about it
The more I doubt that there is such a thing as
Western Civilization. A puritan commercial culture
Was transplanted from Europe to U.S.A. in the 17th Century
American Indians were a civilized people.

I can remember when L.A. had an ideal climate
        "Everybody wants complete privacy in the Hollywood Hills
        for $35 a month," the real estate lady told C.L.T.

She wore this big Marianne Moore garden party hat
rocky face petrified lap-dog. "You don't want to
live over there, Honey, there's Dark Clouds in that
neighborhood."
C. & Shirley escaped to Europe and New Mexico

Bottom of my waterglass, pentagonal crystal
The light changes passing through, bent by glass into color
and we are a rainbow, no matter how we love or hate it
We are beautiful red and black and yellow and brown and white
Maybe a few Swedes or Finns are green in the winter time
If they get cold enough. How can we not be miraculously
Beautiful colors which betray our true nature which is love
And wisdom, compassion and enlightenment,
"Six times three is eighteen"

In Takagamine tiny old lady turns towards a Jizo shrine
Across the street.
A short prayer, umbrella in one hand, the other held up
Before her (gassho) and then bowed very slowly
(She really meant it) first head and neck, and then
The waist, very slowly down and back again.
Jizo-samma certainly must have felt obliged
To attend immediately and in person to that lady's
Children and departed relatives. Being Jizo-samma
He has exactly time and energy and compassion enough
To do exactly that, right now.

can this be straight description or observation
without intending to embarrass or attack anybody,
without waving my arms and yelling

does Mr Gauguin's palette go towards a muddiness
even the tropical pictures are faintly greyed
Fluorescent lights in gallery (Kyoto Municipal Museum)
varnish going bad or the pigments themselves
breaking down? look again

fishpond looks clean
fish are newly polished
Frog-child's baby sister has come to ride her tricycle
orange teddy-bear strapped to her back
the same way her mother carries her
The papa comes to pound a large flat shoe on fishpond rim
fish whirl round in fits, then he scatters crumbs on water
goldfish feed

There is a wonderful kind of writing
Which is never written   NOW
About this moment. It's always done later
And redone until it is perfect.

Praying mantis moored to top of a flower stalk
Grooms itself like a canary
Preens
Two tailfeathers

I wonder whether Wordsworth was subject to fits
Of feeblemindedness or simply had a low opinion
Of his readers?

Bigger mantis upside-down on glass door.
Who else has a face like that:
hammerhead shark another cannibal

Strong mothball smell emanates from English poetry & prose
After the death of Wm Blake . . . or a little before
It is detectable in Keats, Shelley, Byron . . . mothballs
And flannel. Smell of Established Church. Industrialism
And Empire building: same Whiggery rules us now
I've got to go sort out my guts.
"What have you been doing these days?"
Just sorting out my guts: disentangling and
Re-coiling them neatly back in place
The same operation must be performed
Upon the telephone cord, every now and again
Je m'en vais à le Toji, in memory of Koba Daishi
Fleamarket day.

I greet you from the very top of the page

a single branch of stovewood smolders
under the bathtub, the brand of Meleager
still high but able to cook, eat, write, make bath, SWEAT

they ring the bell again I hope all sentient beings
attain complete perfect final enlightenment
which is exactly who I am or not
all my greasy little fingers

coffee-break time down at the Emergency Factory
early in the war, before we all got uniform shot but now
you are trying to confuse me about having my eyes shut
My name is Chauncey M. Depew and it is November 11, 1910
What do you think of that, hey?

STOP IT, I SAY, STOP THIS TRUMPERY MOCKERY
mockery trumpery pink chenille fuzz elephant baby mockery
trumpery trumpery mockery
mongery   freeny-monger?   fundle

Our main difficulty : fear and distrust of freedom
We think it must be carefully measured
Weighed and doled out in discreet quantities
To responsible persons of good character and high
Social standing: people with lots of money which is evidence
Of their reliability and moral quality

Liberty in other hands is "license"

Difficulties compounded by idea of "consent"
And theory of "delegated powers."

Hire specialists to run everything.
But the powers they derive from us
Relieve these governors of all responsibility
Somehow become vast personal wealth—
Fortunes which must be protected from "license" and "the violence of
    the mob"

We find our freedom diminished (KING LEAR)
Delegation a license for the abuse of power
                        say, just what are you trying to prove,
    anyway?
What do I care about proving anything
Only bust chains & shackles that we may slip anchor
Haul-ass away to the making of Paradise
Where now are only fraudulent states, paint-factories
Lies and stinks and wars

One kid put it clear as may be:
"I want America to be magic electrical Tibet"

Or Konzanji, for example, a little NW of the Capital
Absolutely defenseless, abbot's house on pointed mountain
Top, delicate walls
Multitudes of people drifting through it
Footless ghosts, no fingers, empty parkas
The billows of smoke of burnt and burning leaves
The silence, unbroken purity existing in the world

Cuts down impatience
Leaf jewels rage and brilliant silence
Cold flames: Fudo-Myo-o
Carved fire, sculptured flame world net wall
Momentary bird-heads eyes beaks all swirl crimson ray
Beams yellow streaked. He isn't in the fire he's made of it
The light cool zap-energy sword the gentle hat of lotus flower
Big square feet on solid rock Takao-yama

As I looked at them they must see me, flaming
All absurd, film of mistaken proprieties
Culture of dim Oregon farmhouse to burn to dispose of
Instantly
If what is real can be created or destroyed

Clouds move above maples
Change colors we walk beneath
Colored spaces mean something else—
Where in all this tight and elegant disorder. . . . . .

Walk on down Kiyotaki River canyon from Jingoji
Missed the trail, found confluence of Kiyotaki and Hozu rivers
Smooth grey-green cliffs of single rock
Heavy green water, no way back to the Capital
Except by boat, voyage in raging maple colors
Over dragon rocks of dream.
Late extravagant lunch, Arashiyama, Hurricane Ridge

I just reread a little of *The Prelude*
To which I could only reply, "You poor fish."

GOD KNOWS THE SPARROW FELL:
GOD SHOVED HIM.

Let's go visit the tomb of Emperor Murakami
Look at autumn leaves but there light rain starts falling
I had hoped to visit big rock on the hillside, also
But came back home I want my umbrella I want my lunch
       RAIN
serious, wet rain
              discovered the tomb of KOKO TENNO
between the parkway and the trolley track due south of noodle shop
RAY OF FILIAL DUTY who ordered the Ninnaji to be
And the next emperor was first abbot there: UDA TENNO
His Muroji Palace
                 here come the maidens dancing
That song they are singing that song which you shall
Be listening is called "The Song of the Panicled Millet"
In the Chinese classical node

In America we've been fighting each other 100 years
We pretend we're unimaginably rich
But we are poor and afraid of the poor who must become
The Army to defend us against right and wrong
All automatic and impersonal

The Law is The Government
Shall take all your money and kill you
Being completely free and entirely, impartially just

Edgar Allan Poe saw the walls of Plato's Cave
Slowly moving inwards to crush us

Who licks up the juice that runs out at the bottom?

The real shame of America is the lack of an anticlerical
Movement or party. All parties try to compound
With invisible State Protestant Church that theoretically
Doesn't exist. Rubes who think of themselves as
Members in good standing are bilked and robbed.

I got to buy me them eggs.

30 MORE SHOPPING DAYS UNTIL CHRISTMAS!

   "again and again the flames of his inordinate Passion
licked my naked flesh again."

29 MORE SHOPPING DAYS UNTIL CHRISTMAS!

"rolled right over until *I* was over the top of *him* did you ever hear of
such a thing I said Wilbur what on earth are you trying to do and he
was wiggling and shaking and squeezing and panting and saying all

them things over again like he was going crazy until I didn't know whether to send for the doctor or the fire department but he stopped all of a sudden you know how they do and that nasty old stuff all over everything I tell you if I had it to do over again I'd never get married and Wilbur is my third husband"

28 MORE SHOPPING DAYS BEFORE THE FEAST OF THE NATIVITY

"then he turns right around and wants to do it again well I said listen you old goat I've got to get some rest I've got to go shopping tomorrow whether you go to work or not"

27 MORE SHOPPING DAYS UNTIL CHRISTMAS

                        Fred, is that music?

Ah, no, my foolish darling
It is only the roaring of the aged chilling blood
Sluggishly perambulating your brittle veins you forgot
Your bloodpressure pills again, too busy to go out
They brought you three dead sandwiches upon a tray
And coffee, tepid black forbidden coffee
On a tray and you lost your temper on the telephone
And now it echoes in your hollow empty wooden head

           I'm not afraid of you.
           You're nothing but an incubus.

TWENTY-SIX GREATER AND LARGER SHOPPING DAYS BEFORE
  CHRISTMAS

So you're a poet, hey?
Well if you're a poet
Tell me a poem.

Come on, tell me one.

Are you a published poet?

Do you know Nick Crome?

One fine day AG was mad at me and said,
"You're going to be a little old man who smells of kerosene
and sits in the public library every day reading Pliny"

Awoke at quarter-past three A.M. strange wooden clack sound
Later find fallen mud-plaster chunk in *tokonoma*
Puddle of pee with one long black hair in a corner of *benjo* floor

Gloomy gold morning ten A.M. ingest giant lump of bhang
With strawberry jam from Bulgaria (friendly socialist country)
Hot coffee. Things will seem better half an hour from now, OK?
Shut up.

What's the use of having a cold if nobody cares.
Why not simply do something else.
An absolute mystery: how to stop and begin differently.
"Don't be a ninny, Dr Culpepper, all surgery is radical
Hand me that there Gigli-saw. Yes, yes, it all
Connects, have no fear, we can take a tuck in the membrane
If necessary. Try to develop a little more dexterity—
Have you tried practising the piano or the guitar?
Us brain surgeons got to show a little culture.
Quit banging my elbow, nurse."

Fifty years fighting the Bolsheviki
To maintain a 500% profit on every waffle-iron and locomotive
At 499% times are growing difficult, we must try to retrench
At 497½% lay off some of the newer employees the market looks
"Bearish" at 496%   SELL OUT while there's still a chance.
In order to boost profits back to 498%
A "presence" appears in Cambodia

When did the dumb-bunny bomb first hit U.S.A.?
How come everybody appreciated it so much?

THE BAD NEWS INCUBUS SERVICE
                "I'm going to get well right away.
                I'm going to be just fine," the old man said;
                Then his eyes rolled up and his breath stop
                And there he lay dead as a flounder.

Lost again yesterday walking towards Arashiyama
Inconveniently: lunchtime. Several villages,
Tomb of the Emperor Uda, deserted superhighway to Western Hills
I thought of asking somebody, "This the road to China?"
I really knew where I was, I'd been to those mountains
The empty freeway bored and frightened me
Broken highway to a pretty place where I bought expensive noodles
Well, it opened up a space, I could see the distance, for a change
Breathe. Did I miss nine trillion cars, want them to be
On this road with me?

At home, the vegetable supply
A Dutch still-life set on reversed lid of *nabe*
Half a red carrot half a giant radish half a head of hokusai
A completely monumental potato
China will sail across big Zen soup to me

THE BAD NEWS INCUBUS SERVICE
    They peer down through my ceiling
    "Poor old man he's too fat to live much longer"

    Which part of this bothers me most—
    Insincerity, indifference or the fraudulent ceiling?
Voices out of the air the bleak and windy white skull attic
Flat white for lots of light
Hollow wooden head son of a bitch, Homer Matson used to say

I keep trying to remember that this is my life now
What I've got, what I actively chose
Pine tree stone lanterns outside the mason's house imperial tomb
Camellia hedge monkey-slide tree
And the responsibility for learning two languages (which
I evade) and dim insistences of two others in the background
Sanskrit and Tibetan.   awk!

WHY DID I LAUGH TO-NIGHT?
NO VOICE.

At the foot of the stonewall Fukuoji Jinsha
Somebody took leave of her shoes;
There they are.
Red.

Strangely enough I find that I'm all right
Nothing's really wrong with me, there's food
Payday will be Thursday the pleasure of looking at
A tiny mountain of low-grade amethyst
Almost the color of gas flame cooking buckwheat noodles
(kerosene is on the way)
The cold weather is neither monster nor prodigy
I seem to survive it (Vitamin C) in spite of paranoia
(Vitamin B-complex shortages?).
In winter the air is cold as it is hot in summer

But I never can understand the idea

All too soon I must leave these beauties
And come away to heaven's boring towers of golden flapping
Snowy wings and halo bright star crown
No more to see your sexy frown and freckles
            ("I can't find my mirror!
            I can't find my things!")
So that when you've at last arrived there too
Shall we bleak and holy strangers distant forgiving nod and smile?
But soon you'll be asking me, "How do I look?
Is my halo all right? I know my wings are all slaunch-wise
Along the trailing edge." (Preen, preen.) "I wish I had
My mirror, Kids! I wish I had all my things Oh well
I don't care please hold me I want you to hang onto me a while."

Torn paper fake mountains become three-dimensional
Transparent crystals. Bushes and trees all
Barbered and shaved plaques of tourmaline, emerald
They used to tell me I must apply myself
Work hard and don't be lazy
But what I must learn is to accomplish everything
Which has nothing to do with work.
Work is what an instrument or engine does.
We say a crystal changes white light to green
Breaks light into rainbow, scatters it

Focuses to burning point. The crystal does
Nothing. Its shape and structure make all
The difference. Think of transistors and lasers.
In order to make this day great
Yesterday must be altered

Rain I must wear overcoat muffler and bamboo umbrella
Thinking of monkey tribes on Hieizan and Iwatayama
Wet & freezing I hope they're finding food
Lovely bronze-green fur, defenseless eyes
They run if you stare at them:
Fixed gaze prepares for pounce crunch fangs of death
All monkies everywhere look worried all the time
Eyes and faces, "Oh God, what next. Me?"
Lots of instructions wasted

Go down town and argue with the bank
Fall, as leap
Fred?
Yesterday afternoon they said
They'd pay in the morning.
This morning they say
They'll pay in the afternoon

Raving hot sunshine two days before Christmas
                    BAFFLEMUTE
& so to Osaka.

Beguile me with all them blandishments again!
Cursus:
The hotel falls. The false hotel.
Enter One in the character of a false hotel. He speaks:

MALEMUTE!

BEZOAR!

TREMENDULATE!

FACTION.

CUCURBITE.

Pantages.
TRASHMULE.
finger

A man in a black suit stands at the entrance to the tomb
Of the Emperor Enyu, catty-corner from my front door
He bellows like a bull at irregular intervals

A man steps out the front door of his house
He says (in French), "Again, the same thing."

Radio gives me German actors performing *Faust*

I'm reminded of *Hudibras*
The triumph of commercial middle class
Chanted in paltry quatrains. *Toujours la même chose.*
A little chocolate tomb for a dead marischino cherry

Coffeeshop sugarbowl another compromise
Picture of childish French sailor
"English" inscription (sans-serif letters)
               "anchortheway"
A lisping *matelot*? *Encore*, the way?
"Encore, vos nerfs."

Leaps & bounds
Ponderous numbers to confine
Limit the flower
               A measured compromise
"I didn't get her cherry but I got the box it came in."
The flower goes beyond the edge of its petals
The poem runs past the edge of the paper
Teeth I don't have anymore hurt me today

Today I started late and quit early
And accomplished everything, but the next day was
Marred by fits of rage, mental confusion
Lapses of memory. Olson dead in New York
Jack dead in Florida. Today I am going to take more:
Smoked some and ate some

OM.   AH.   HUM.

in five sacred colors
I woke up a couple of times during the night
High with lights and music behind the eyes
This morning I am cured and know who and where I'm at

Why should I go to Europe to look at
Several million nervous white folks
My very own relatives there they are
Totally uncivilized, fingering and puzzling over
The ruins of Western Civilization
I feel closer to that culture which our ancestors
Destroyed . . . megalithic builders initiated in mushroom
Mysteries at Crete, Eleusis, New Grange

In this capital we also fumble with ruins of high culture
But feelings of antique propriety keep heavy sway
Over family, marriage, feudal obligations to a chief
The life of the Capital goes by in tight pants
Or on horseback brilliant silk *hakama*
Brocade *karaginu* gleaming lacquer hat

Summer's dead leaves philaudering into dusty moss
Like melting Dracula.
            (PHILAUDERING. *Mot imaginaire de l'auteur.*)
The soul extractors are here.

Edgar W. Tomczyk of Lima, Ohio, will now attempt
To drive a 35-ton Caterpillar tractor through
Two inches of boiling water from which he will escape
Absolutely unharmed!
              (oops.)
Rupert Scanlon of Great Falls, Montana will now . . .

The world (and I)
Barge past the sun
Glass on stove's fuel-gauge reflects
The sun onto north wall twenty feet away
The passage of Time, the zooming of the earth
Can be witnessed as a disc of light
Sliding over dots of mud plaster sand
Other goop embedded in the surface

Daitokuji celebration day still echoes in my head
Sound of manhole-cover falling flat on stone floor
The rainy maples at Koto-In.
Last night wild boar for supper
Shakuhachi music over snowy torrent
BOTAN NABE, Peony Cassoulet
So far north of the Capital the road is only paved
When it becomes (five seconds) mountain village mainstreet
among *sugi* trees ordinary dirt in the canyons
But the people speak *Kyoto-ben*.
BOTAN garden of Daitokuji monastery

Manhole-cover clang and crash
Big pair of cymbals, thin brass with center bowl
Broad-rim soup dishes B L A S H !

Everybody dolled up in brocade bib and tucker
Chinese canal-boat shoes, Nootka shaman hats
To exceed wisdom and ignorance escape skull chain
(Juzu beads I saw today each bead a white head-bone
Apparently impossible although there's enough space
Between bone crystals to drive a truck through)

There's not an owl in the world who thinks or knows
"I am an owl." Not one who knows there's a man called
Slotkin who knows more about owls and the owl trade
Than any owl. I wonder though,
Can Professor-Doktor Slotkin eat mice and fly.

Kyoto 6 P.M. News:
Somebody left a pistol in a raincoat in a taxi on
Higashiyama (Eastern Mountain) Road

New York Buddha Law:
All sentient beings will be brought
To complete final perfect enlightenment
If you will write a letter to *The New York Times*
Condemning Ignorance, Desire and Attachment.

Almost all Americans aged 4 to 100
Have the spiritual natures of Chicago policemen.
Scratch an American and find a cop. There is no
Generation gap.

I sit in the north room
Look out across the floor into the garden
12½ tatami mats the pleasure of contemplating them
They are beautiful and they aren't mine.
Present appearance of quiet neutral emptiness
Books, music, pictures, letters, jewels, machines
Buddha statues and other junk all hidden away
As if inside my head (think of the closets
As memory banks) Wooden ceilings pale orange
Floors the color of wheat straw, light-grey paper
Colored mountains near the bottom cover the fusuma
That divide rooms hide closets. Glass and white paper
Shoji screens two garden ends of the house north and south

Heavy floral designs of Michoacan
(Have you ever considered going THERE to live)
O flowers more lovely than wine
Adonis and/or Dionysus . . .
". . . only one note and it a flat one . . ."
"Only a rose
For you." (That was a long time ago.)

(unique abyss)

"I'll go along

With a smile & a song

For anyone . . ." all this was

Copyrighted maybe 1911 "ONLY A ROSE

FOR YOU!"

So long ago I was a prisoner still and other people

Made everything happen good bad & indifferent

"Control yourself!" they said

To survive continuous neural bombardment

Meningeal bubbles twenty years after—

Now I make things happen

These thin brass domes and birds of ice

Cheap fruity cries pop

There's your tricycle (from Jimmy Broughton's movie,

Mother's Day)

tricycle from the Isle of Man

Three legs running

"The Shinto emblem showing three comma-shaped figures in a whirl

symbolizes the triad of the dynamic movements of musubi . . ." — Jean

Herbert

Athenian abyss   Tarquin Old Stairs   off the steep

edge of town   Delphi something else

a friend writes from Eleusis: "nothing here

but a vacant lot . . . factories in the distance"

"Those caves of ice"

,

(large comma)

"JA!" Mr C. Olson used to say so the word

Had a big walrus mustache laden with fresh beer foam

Flowers have great medicinal virtue

I decide not to go to town until Wednesday

Buy *Time* to read at Asahi Beer Hall, not have to teach

I just now caught bright future glimpse

Of myself on Wednesday: Long green coat

Orange beard glasses completely distracted

By trauma of trying to talk Japanese to the waitress

Out of patience out of breath wrestling to break

Strong wool British overcoat stranglehold

flowers and vegetables

                    maybe they will change my mind

The light is different because it's a different season

              (Audumb in New York)

usual garden uniform green moss a pleasure.

In spring unexpected crocus and lily and tulip

Crash through it—surprising shapes and colors

Western Civilization rigid and tyrannical
But it also teaches necessity for objective examination
Of the organization and also provides all kinds of suggestions
How to alter the works. Mr Karl Marx wrote a book
All by his lonesome in the British Museum. (Shhh!)

I've read the trial and death of Socrates
Lots of times. When it hits me right I can cry
Other days I wonder why it took the Government so long
To catch up with him. Nothing happened
To Plato, there he sits, writing.

Homer and The Classics burnt at Appomattox
Confucius enjoyed a vogue as originator of jokey sayings, 1939

30:IV, 7:55 A.M. Unknown quantity & quality LSD
7:21 P.M. head full of million-watt light
Hangs from the ceiling, old China dome
Newly uncovered. Dirty but thin, hard and shiny.
Far-away midge on quiet *tatami*.
Many amperes and micro-watts weeded the garden
Picked it up by one end and shook it
Like the dog's dirty blanket, *flooch! flooch!*
And resettled it softly down over the shrubs and bugs
Lots of discoveries underneath
All miraculous and alive

The Capital more than usually full of foreigners—
Expo '70, Osaka. Americans at first imagine
Japan is extension of Cincinnati suburbs
Amazed and outraged to find everything here
In careful and complete control of people who don't
Speak English, occupied (somewhat aggressively) with
Being very Japanese.

That is the funny man's house over there.
That's where the funny man lives.
Keep away.
Hair.   Hair.   Hair.   Hair.   Hair.

THE JOURNAL OF JOHN GABRIEL STEDMAN 1744–1797,
                    "June 9 (1795) . . . the Apollo gardens,
Marylebone, Madagascar bat as big as a duck . . .
June 24 . . . How dreadful London; where a Mr. B— declared
openly his lust for infants, his thirst for regicide,
and believes in no God whatever.
. . . August . . . Met 300 whores in the Strand. . . . Saw a mermaid
(. . . September . . .) All knaves and fools and cruel to the
excess. Blake was mobb'd and robb'd."

A friend wrote from Kent, Ohio, last year
      "The Midwest is full of people who want to write poetry
      and want to listen to it."
This year the National Guard, weeping with pity and fright

Kill four students, firing "into the mob"
Nobody cared. Nobody remembers the Korean "Police Action"
Nobody will remember our "Advisory Mission" to Indo-China
                    why are they doing it
Why are they
                    oh, never mind am I supposed to judge them
Don't you remember being high and weeding the garden
And whatever is really beautiful can't be destroyed
We can't get our hands on it,

                    ". . . The truly great
    Have all one age, & from one visible space
    Shed influence! They, both in power and act,
    Are permanent, and Time is not with them,
    Save as it worketh for them, they in it."
                    —S. T. Coleridge, "To William Wordsworth"

Endless weedy babble comes away easily
The flowers feel different, having been intentionally
Placed by living fingers which I also feel
Just think of it as a large allegorical painting
Nude figures, red velvet drapery, white marble
"Classical Architecture" (Parthenon Bank of Chemical Pantheon Library)
                    America Devouring Her Own Young

(The soldiers are also our children, we've lied to them, too
Americanism, Baseball, Commerce, Democracy, Education, Fanaticism

Golf, Home Economics,

                    ignorance

The complete college curriculum

Then put them into uniform and turn them loose with guns

To kill "hate-filled long-hair dirty dope-fiend Com/Symp")

Nobody cares because nothing really happened

It was on the TV, everybody will get up

Wash off the catsup, collect union wages & go home

Nobody cares, nobody thinks anything about it

No thoughts at all; a succession of needs and little raunchy

Schemes. "They should have killed a few hundred more—

All a Communist plot to move Blacks into suburbs

Turn over the country to freeloaders, dope-fiend hippy queers"

The American Revolution was a tax-dodge

Dreamed up by some smart Harvard men

Who got some good out of it.

A few of their high-society friends also scored

Russian Revolution a strictly ugly downtown proposition

The Great Unwashed on a rampage. No reference to mystical

Rights to Life & pursuable happiness guaranteed by

Eighteenth Century rationalist Deity in curly wig

Old man potters down the lane singing

Stops to search the roadside flowers and weeds

For some particular leaf that he puts in plastic bag
Of greens. Last night's old man, KONDO Kenzo
(80-some odd years) performed the Nō of *Motomezuka*
Acting a young girl and her ghost frying in hell
We all kept waiting for him to stumble, collapse
Fall off the stage disintegrate
But the longer we watched the clearer it became:
The stage, the entire theater might collapse much sooner
Fall to sand and rust and splintered beams
Mr Kondo would still be there singing and dancing
Every fold of his costume in place five hundred years

It pleases folks in Washington D.C. to imagine
The Russian Revolution is going to flop any minute now
(After fifty years) the insurgent Bolsheviki will be put down
The dear Tsar restored as modern constitutional monarch
(We did it in Tokyo, didn't we?) and the Patriarch of
The Church will crown him in St Basil's while the Don
Cossack Choir (beards and gold brocades) chant Slavonic
Liturgies in full color satellite TV an example
To the benighted everywhere, if only we will pay
Just a little bit more and hire a few more FBI men

A few inches of adhesive tape seals the mouth
But it is hard to get rid of the idea of liberty
After forty years of war Asia still exists,
Not to mention the Viet Cong

And quite different from the plans of Washington
Or Moscow or the Vatican. (Napoleon said, "China . . .
Sleeping giant. I shudder to think what happen
When he wake . . .")

Adhesive tape in Federal Court
Nothing wrong with the System
You'll get a chance to talk later.
Federal Court held together with gum arabic
And Chicago cops

Nara has a great magical feeling
The city no longer exists, the first capital
Restored fragments of temples, carefully excavated
Site of Imperial Palace in the rice fields
Like Olson I've been writing about the wrong town?
                "Worcester! I'm from Worcester!
                All this about Gloucester . . .
                I've been writing about the wrong town
                All this time!" (Vancouver, 1963)

Kent State, Jackson State, There was no reason to kill them
Fusillade into an unarmed crowd
Of children.
I can't forgive us for feeding them
to the Bears currently raiding Wall Street

Painless Extraction time again
Squeezing water out of the stocks
Blood out of the suckers
Everybody hopes to catch a nice gob of the goo
But there's never quite enough

Didn't you hear about the reservations? You were supposed
To phone ahead for reservations. In advance.
Never quite enough, the Official Party had
To be served first.
Never quite enough
Because it was planned that way.

My grandmother used to say, "And so he was left
S.O.L."
I asked her, "What's that mean?"
"Certainly out of luck."
Those that's got, gets. Them that ain't is S.O.L.

       "Oh, the coat and the pants
       Do all of the work
       But the vest gets all the gravy!"

We complain of Tiberius in the White House
But consider: Caligula
Waits fretfully in some provincial capital

CAPITAL REMOVED TO FUKUHARA (Kamo no Chōmei reporting)
6th month, 1180—

"To the north the land rose up high along a ridge of hills and to
the south sloped down to the sea. The roar of the waves made a con-
stant din and the salt winds were of a terrible severity. The palace was
in the mountains, and, suggesting as it did the log construction of the
ancient palaces, was not without its charms. . . . The manners of the
capital had suddenly changed and were now exactly like those of rustic
soldiers."

Oregon City by the papermill falls of Willamette
There's Dr John McLoughlin's big white house
Retired magnificence of Hudson Bay Co.
Benefactor of our Pioneer Ancestors
John Jacob Astor ran him out of business
Washington Irving described all but the money

Where was the capital: Champoeg,
Oregon City, Portland, Salem.
The money is in Portland the university in Eugene
The capital in Salem: Life Along The Willamette River?
                    now a stink-hole
Paper-puke sulphur trioxide and mercury
The lesser towns contribute only garbage and human excrement

The Capitol's great brass dome warping
Melting in the flames

Hand-carved oak and myrtle and walnut panelling
State House in the park, toy stage set, blazing
A lost art, my father used to say. Nobody knows
How to do that any more.
Palaces by Vanbrugh, mansions and watergates of Inigo Jones
Gardens by Capability Brown
                    blazing
"Sept. 2, a lamentable fire. . . . the wind being eastward blew
clouds of smoke over Oxon the next day . . . the moon was dar-
kened by clouds of smoak and looked reddish. The fire
or flame made a noise like the waves of the sea."
So says Anthony à Wood.

Yet there are still remaining
Shosoin, parts of the Horyuji, Yakushiji, Toshodaiji
The capital disappeared around them. Byodoin and Muroji
Parts of Daigoji too far away from the battlefields
And from carelessness, perhaps. These can still be seen,
In spite of earthquake, ambition, silliness
The thousand Buddhas at Sanjusangendo, the others at
The Toji, survived though the city was flattened
Eight or ten times in a row

Jack used to say,
"Some day you and Gary and Allen and me
Will all be old bums under a bridge,
Down by the railroad tracks. We'll say,

Remember when we was all out there in Californy,
Years ago?"

Gentle rain from grey-black lump clouds
Fine pale blue sky
Three-color cat sits on weedpile
Near but not under the largest branch of Mt Koya pine

All I can say this morning is a dance
Which can't be recorded here
A wish to be free from orders, notions, whims
Mine or other people's
Waiting for the laundry delivery man
Waiting for 95 liters of kerosene
Chrysanthemum yellow starfish tube-
Foot petals

Ancient Orient! Shortest route to the forebrain
Through olfactory lobes. Longest way round is
The shortest way home. A little trip
Through the Anima Mundi, now show
Now currently appearing a persistent vision
When it happens at the correct speed
But if you get too close it is only
Patterns of light
Drop candy and try to follow it

Creates new place and time. Looking up
I see blank staring faces
Reflecting steady silver glow. Silence.

Under the bright umbrella, University of British Columbia
Beer on the terrace of the Faculty Club Allen & Bob
Straightening out something complicated,
Olson sighing the while, "I hear you. One, four, three.
I hear you. One, four, three. Minor's Ledge Light.
One, four, three. I LOVE YOU. One, four, three, Minor's
Ledge Light. You remember, don't you Bob. One, four, three
I LOVE YOU—what better way to remember?"

Do intelligent questions get interesting answers.
All I know is
Every time I get mixed up with rich folks
It costs me all the money I have in my pocket

                    CURIOUS ELISION
                    LORD, HAVE MERCY UPON US

Michaelangelo/Cole Porter Variations DAY & NIGHT;
NIGHT & DAY, waking and sleeping
That's what that's all about
A man with titties like a woman
A woman with muscles like a man

"To Europe?"

. . . .

"I must have adorned it with a strange
grimace, but my inspiration had been right.
To Europe . . ."

—Henry James.

Pierre who?

"coming & going"

"well if you'd got drunk and
climbed up to the top of the door
and took off all your clothes
and passed out cold
how would Y O U look?

No matter how far we travel
We find most of the world living as quasi-civilized
Nomads among polished marble ruins of great cultures
The quality of life and the meaning of these remains
Are quite imperfectly known to us, no matter how skillfully
We parse the verbs of lost languages
All ignorantly we project our own savagery & cannibalism
Upon societies and individuals who were
Our civilized ancestors

Christ now returns under the name U.S.A.
Rages wild across the earth to avenge himself

Napalm and nuclear bombs for every insult
Every prick of thorn crown
"Not peace but a sword"   (Curious elision.)
Lays about him burning and smashing
Murdering the Sea,

       The war continues because it is profitable.
       It's making good money for those who had
       Money to invest in it from the beginning

Curious elision for all who did not.

All of a sudden it became as if nothing had happened
And that was the end.

Babies we creep out of water sack
Hid there by young men
Old we slide into firebox
Drift up the flue to heaven

A natural history. A narrow escape.

What happened. Walked to local coffeeshop
Tomato juice. Start home *via* Ninnaji templegrounds
People chanting in front of magic Fudo spring
I went to look at the Mie-do, then realized
I was sick or at least beleaguered by creep vibrations

Clearly time for magical cure.
I poured water over Fudo his rocky image
Chanted his mantra and bowed. I also rubbed
Magic water on my head. Old lady caretaker
Delighted;   she said I had done well and wished
For my rapid recovery.

To enforce the cure I visited Fudo spring at
Kiyomizudera, the Kwannon and other Buddhas there
Expensive tempura lunch with view of Chion In
The Eastern Mountains and a glimpse of Momoyama Castle
Glimpse has a marvelous sound like limpkin and Temko

"That Fudo a good old boy he from Texas!"

Shinshindo Coffee house brick fountain,
Stone, tree, new leaves, now a new electrical
Garden lamp on metal pole, as in Mrs Blah's patio/barbecue "area"
Chagrin Falls, Ohio. The latest incarnation of
The Frog Child tries to ride minute red tricycle
That groans and squeals. Delicious croissants.
I can still feel happy here. How come.

I'm too fond of eggplant ever to be allowed into Heaven
But imagine celestial *brinjal—   aubergines du paradis*!
ANACHRONISM:
                    a) homesick for one of
                         the chief cities of Ohio

b) process for correcting chromatic
aberration in camera and other lenses

One of the most wonderful and magical actions
We can perform: Let something alone. Refuse
To allow yourself the pleasure of messing it up.
The thing appears to want adjusting, improving,
Cleaning up &c. APPEARS so to us
But as a collection of "event particles"
A section of the Universe as a noisy morning &c
Leave it alone. Don't tamper with it.

Free of that poor-ass Oregon down-home history
As this clear water streaming over head eyes face
I can see hollyhocks ten feet high sideways
To go and to stay illusory
I flee pale music
                    (I know what I'm doing, NIGHT & DAY)
I flee Death's pale music
                    (Well, what?)
Fleeing Death's proud music,
"Get up out of there," my father used to say,
"You can't sleep your life away.
People die in bed." But I am tired of all the world
With notebook and pen I hurl myself deep among
The dopey sheets to bed, and lock the gates!
Shopping among the sand at the bottom of a birdcage
Every grain a universe designed by Walter Lantz

Nonskid never-fail plastic whose colors fade
All surfaces dim and grubby all of them scraped
Minutely scored cracked and flawed
Material impervious to most chemicals
Resistant to ordinary wear
Allegorical painting: CUPIDITY DECEIV'D BY ADVERTISING
The canary in residence is terribly
Intelligent and infested with mites.

"Rooty-toot-toot" was the sound of the little .44
Frankie wasted her faithless lover
Whenever I asked people what all that meant
They said "Never mind"—
"Row the boat, Norman, row!"

Hot weather erodes my powers
At the Ishiyamadera, small room with bo-leaf window
(For the viewing of the moon, the priest explains.)
She looks at the moon through that window that you see
Over there. She is now a wax dummy with a face
That exhibits what the Japanese think of as "refined"
Features. All dressed up in Heian court robes
Long black hair down her back. In the antechamber
A smaller dummy represents girl-child attendant
Grinding ink at a large inkstone
The figure of Murasaki holds a writing brush

And a long piece of paper. Her head has begun to turn
Away from the writing to observe the moon
And quite likely to remark upon the song of the uguisu
Scholars, Japanese and Western, say she never did,
Never was here a minute. The priest shows
A sutra copied out in Murasaki's own handwriting
Here's the very inkstone that she used.
There is the moonlight window.

Dog days, ten years, I try to remember your face
You disappear, all my head can see
Are two paintings and drawing in red ink
Whatever else I've done with my life
Amounts to nothing

But inside the lantern a white speckled black beetle
Not quite as large as a rice-bird gives
Complete performance of *Siegfried* all alone

I am a hunting and gathering culture
The Moselle wine-boat sails over icy Delaware
On gossamer wing through the woods to Skye
(Hurrah for Miss Flora MacDonald)
Under the shadow of those trees
Edge of typhoon sudden rain
Shelter at Basho's Rakushisha hut

Green persimmons next door to Princess Uchiko her tomb
(Famous for her Chinese poems, first priestess of Kamo Shrine)
Under the shadow of those trees, waiting for the boat
Cythère

POÉME IMMENSE ET DRÔLETIQUE
    Night morning Greyhound bus NEVADA have a new driver
    all on different schedules
                "quel sentiment. quelle
                delicatesse"
    Who shall be first to arrive?

Chaos is an ideal state
None of us has ever experienced it
We are familiar with confusion, muddle and disarray
True disorder is inaccessible to us

        ". . . the sense of beauty rests gratified
        in the mere contemplation or intuition,
        regardless whether it be a fictitious Apollo
        or a real Antinous."
                —Coleridge, Notebook, 1814.

"White noise"
Brownian motion
Spinthariscope
"Cosmic rays"

I look out for a moment from behind the Great Book Mountain

Feeling like Lemuel Gulliver

      (this isn't exactly what

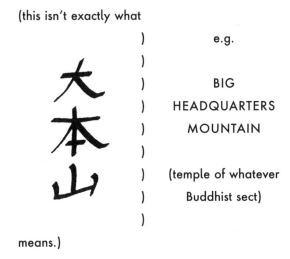

)   e.g.

)

)   BIG

)   HEADQUARTERS

)   MOUNTAIN

)

)   (temple of whatever

)   Buddhist sect)

)

means.)

DISTRACTION

assemblage of eggs green onions butter and

amethyst crystals on top of the kitchen cabinet

A mountain of quartz 喝 crystals 水晶

A whole set, (90 yen worth) of red beans

Gone up in smoke while I rummage three dictionaries

Four different texts in three incomprehensible languages

喝

Minestrone

For all sentient beings

金昔

get me out of here! Bail me
out of the WORD OCEAN

"I wish to God
I never see your face
Nor heard your lion tongue"

And so knocked over my drink
I now have a pantsfull of cold sweet coffee
Hop up out of the way and white shirt all stained
On account of G. M. Hopkins:
    "What do then? how meet beauty? Merely meet it; own,
    Home at heart, heaven's sweet gift; then leave, let that alone.
    Yea, wish that though, wish all, God's better beauty, grace."

Whatever any of that means (TO WHAT SERVES MORTAL BEAUTY?)
I am suddenly spastic brainless
Flailing arms and feet
Complete total mess. Rush home. Underwear
Hair and wristwatch and all pockets
Full of coffee syrup, take a bath to get rid of it
Before the ants can find me

Poor Hopkins imagined he had it completely under control
Set framed and crystallized

It all explodes iced coffee in ten directions,
Three worlds. He had to be a priest
Poetry was some other trip forced on him
Squirting out every nozzle, pore and orifice

I must have been reaching for my notebook
With both hands and several more
I wanted to copy that message here
Some arm and fingers held the Hopkins book,
Yet other hands reaching for pen—did I yell,
I wonder—which of these hands arms elbows
Knocked the glass *towards* me?
                    coffee and sugar leaping in
                    capillaries of my brain

Coffee or sleep thick and sweet
Heavy chocolate hours of morning
Deliberately. And now 10:30 A.M. washed and broken away
From books and music I sit with my feet melting
In bright invisible mountain water that lies above
Brown chocolate mud and fir needles and little sticks
Two inches or twenty feet below—impossible to judge
Because of stillness and clarity of water
Smooth and heavy as cloth of cold
Black transparent stream,
                    anyway I thought that was the reason

SWAMI VIVEKANANDA: ". . . Like an insane person I ran out of our
house. He asked me, 'What do you want?'
I replied, I want to remain immersed in sa-
madhi. He said: 'What a small mind you
have! Go beyond samadhi! Samadhi is a
very trifling thing.'"

In the capital the commonest materials—
mud, plain paper, a couple boards and a bush and a rock,
A handful of straw—stuff we think of as worthless
Throw it away, certainly not to use for building a house
But set here in proportion, in specific spatial relation
An order of decorum and respect for themselves
Out of nothing at all, a house and garden
That can't last more than ten minutes
Very quietly stays forever

Here at the edge of town people visit me
As they used to hike up Sauk Mountain
Or to the Sourdough Lookout. They sidle up
And say, "Ain't you kind of lonely
Up here all alone?" I have to lie and say
"Sometimes," because they look injured & rejected
If I say "No." The truth is that living
In remote and foreign places takes a lot of
Work, every day, no time to feel sad and friendless

The neighborhood barber watches my hair walk by
Jealously. So much for
The Law of Karma.

Where is Los Angeles? Where IS Los Angeles
In among the minnie-bombs & maxi-toons
Cloud, altocumulus, as appears above islands
Far at sea.
O California lardy-dar

What is California, nothing but South Alaska
    "See how CANADA comes me cranking in
    And cuts me from the best of all my land
    A huge half-moon, a monstrous cantle out . . ."
                        Northern Chile
I didn't know what I was getting into
Until it was too late and now I am a   F R E A K !
        O California!
  A   G R E A T   B I G   F R E A K
        (ugh!)

almost white granite with little stars
Juniper trees in high California
Recollected at a great distance
Everyplace else forgot
Thinking "Moon still important at
The capital" and "L'AIDE-MEMOIRE DE LA VRAIE LOI"

An awfully large number of us
Had our heads bent with nowhere theories
Presented in beguiling books
Marx and Lenin, Freud and Jung, Churchill and Lord Keynes
Kafka and Kierkegaard,
In spite of or on account of which
Becoming cannon-fodder for sadist politicians
Patients of expensive quacks. How come.

    "In short, he bid me goe to the Fountain head,
    and read Aristotle, Cicero, Avicenna, and did call
    the Neoteriques shitt-breeches."
        —Aubrey's *Life of Wm. Harvey*

I suspect you can be as nutty with a head full
Of Greek and Latin, but maybe less easily imposed upon
And perhaps a little less dangerous?

Anthony à Wood, *Life & Times*: "In this month [May] was
            to be seen at the Fleur de luce [*inn at Oxford*]
            a brasen head that would speak and answer."

Neighbor's new iron gate sound
Bones of my right arm and elbow.

Always. America. Always a line of people
Ten or fifteen of them, all very smart

Waiting at the madhouse door to their parents' bedroom
Walking in their sleep—what time is it.
What does "dromedary" actually mean.
Cancel my subscription to TRAK Service.

Banana trees now at their best
But the most exciting green is rice in the paddy
Just beginning to produce ears of grain
Middle of August, shimmering subliminal green waves
And secret power-vibes
Maybe high quality emeralds can do
A similar job? However, the rice is alive
To be eaten later or brewed into *sake*
And so transports us out of Oregon skull
The sea's defective music as a passing bull
Suborns eleven
I can tell.

"AWAY, THOU FONDLING MOTLEY HUMOURIST!"

An overdose of America
Money and too many decibels

      Miss Janice climb up
      On a white snow horse
      Never climb down any more

O Sunflower, mouldy with grime, &c
Waste and want. Sung flower?

An overdose of pure London
Took Jimi Hendrix away,

  " . . . rueful again the piteous bagpipe went
  O bag-pipe thou didst steal my heart away"
    ("Fled music is the sweetest
    My Fair Lady")
"Of late two dainties were before me plac'd"

John Keats also lost

  "that's going to be him, see, how
  Monkey Face slips down over Great Seal
  Eyes and proliferation of curves
  From working too fast before the epipyroxylin
  Cools"

    Yukio MISHIMA, novelist, playwright, actor,
    Suicide by elegant Japanese tradition

Produces the effect of an infinite territory
What?
With only one possible neighboring color
What? Monads?

No, there's, no, no, not nomads, no, no

That idea was discredited, can't work, David Hume

What about volvox colonies

Universe of spheres containing spheres

All individual, all neighbors with independent spheres

Inside, so beautifully Buchsbaum

Never mourned, no eyes, what

FERN

the effect of uninterrupted acceleration (however famil-
iar the track) certain contact-plates prepare trees light
up animals move and sing laugh in the dark

EMERALDS

*

GONE

*

I drink bad expensive Italian wine

Beside the Kamo River. They say

You've taken a new lover. Passengers

On Sanjo Bridge Hieizan profile

Now all marvelously smudged by pen of hispid friend

Bottled somewhere near Florence, I expect

All the customers in here will rise and applaud

When I leave this place. They have been profoundly

Edified by the spectacle of a certified FOREIGNER
Gobbling up a pizza with his fingers
Drinking a bottle of wine without falling off his chair
A scene of life at the capital

I haven't been drunk for a long time
Reminds me of you, before we all
Became dope-friends. When was your last trip,
I went cuckoo on LSD the 30th of April

There's already been a great deal said about wine
And I'm reading the faggoty part of *The Anthology*
Thinking of you instead of naked boys
Curious elision. I've drunk 0.475 liter of "chianti"
Much too fast. Antinori. (Antenor was a mythological
What did he do?)

Hieizan sadder and smaller than Mt Koya
But still a mountain in several senses
Even though they drive buses to it
The buses go home at night; the trees take over
You can step out of temples into rhododendron flowers
                         ruins
Path which Mas Kodani followed seven days in rain
Priest robes, shaman hat, straw sandals too small,
Would wild monkeys attack him? Reciting HANNYA SHINGYO
Wherever stone marker on the trail shows where temple was

What was I saying. Talking to you.
A slow green train leaves for Uji
A slow green train arrives from Osaka
Immediately departs. I just realized that all I've said
For the past ten years was addressed to you
Simple and flat as that.

Kite! not the toy, a living bird
Sails above Kamogawa, that same Goddess
In worldly form dips and swings
Far below a northbound airplane
"KEE-REE!"
              "The hawk flies up to heaven"

I have to write this at home with a new pen
I pitched the other into the Kamo
The moment it lifted from writing "-REE!"
To the complete consternation and horror
Of the other guests

              Now this Antenor has a curious history.
              Brother-in-law to Priam, King of Troy,
              he betrayed the Palladium to the Greeks
              that they might capture the Capitol. He
              escaped with his family to found New Troy
              in Italy (Venice or Padua?) the father of
              the prophet, Laocoön. Pious Aeneas founded

a second Troy at Rome. Noble Brutus founded
Troynovaunt, *alias* London, capital of the world?

"It is said in the Book of Poetry, 'The hawk flies up
to heaven; the fishes leap in the deep.'"

Horror & chagrin of other patrons
Who carefully preserve their papers, ink and brushes and ink
Stones in elegant lacquer boxes.
Writing is a serious action presided over by a god,
Tenjin-O-Mi-Kami-Samma, at the Kitano Shrine

All these worlds change faster than I can tell you
I have this reading & writing habit which I cultivate
Excessively, perhaps, little time for anything else
Although it's fun to ride the Osaka zipper
Forty-eight minutes for 65 miles
Fast asleep to Yodoyabashi branch Bank of America

Sound asleep we leave the capital rainy night
(Boats which children might have made from apple boxes)
Passengers remaining awake rattle their beads
Call on Amida Buddha and Kwannon to save them

Under the cushions and the *goza* matting
I feel the planks bulge as they slide
Snail foot over boulders and rocks

Far in the middle of the river
Safe and dry sound asleep left Sōō Temple, Yamazaki Bridge
At sundown. Early morning waken to shouts
Boatswarm harbor of Naniwa
Thanks to Gods of Sumiyoshi!

Vegetable nerves
Cold noodle time in the Capital
I got to kick my coffee habit.
Anybody seen my tranks? Remind me
How is Steve Carey?

Haloes
Which the angels left behind
Empty niches where holy saints once
Hand-hewn bases for noble columns: garden decorations
Wintermin (Chlorpromazine hydrochloride, 12.5 mg tabs)
    "Motion sickness, vomiting of pregnancy, potentiating
    effects on hypnotics and analgesics, psychoneurosis
    such as anxiety neurosis, bed-wetting, Pollakiuria."

        did you say "Bum trip"
        or "dumb trip"?

Gardening.
Cleaning the o-furo
Spilling the tea I'm going crazy

Sweating and freezing the sky overcast
Hot wooly clouds shove my head under cold water
Dry it off and start over.
The barber's lady assistant shaved
The rostra of my ears

Before this day is out a great pink peony
Shall have bloomed (note expensive leather hollyhock!)
All pink all
Carved out of the interior
                of my eye
                    (BRANCUSI)

I've won every marble
Now I'm running mad
Gardening. Little circular trips.
Dirt produces infinite weed babble
My hands know it; my eyes blunk out, don't see
Hands read garden

I can catch the sun if I stop grabbing and
Turn my hand over. The sun falls into my open
Palm a sun much larger than we first imagined
We live in its atmosphere

If you want something hold out an empty hand

Newly opened peony delicate camphor perfume box

If you want a poem find a blank page

As if America were the final utterance
Of the human race: A culmination and the end
Land of the greed and the home of the knave?
Most of my compatriots will never learn
That "the human race" is not the same thing as
"White Protestant population of USA"
That "civilization" means neither "Metropolitan Opera Co."
Nor "modern American hospital"

I'd like to catch up with whoever it was
That placed these weird creatures forever in my cure
Crowned my goofy dome with red hat
Mitre and magic oils
This isn't my job; I mustn't resign

Kite wheels above
Bridge of the Changing Moon
                        that's the end of that.

My head so packed with contradictory orders and
Theories and "categorical imperatives" and messages
From various power systems and from beyond the tomb

It's no wonder that my eyes don't focus and I'm
Plagued by asthma, headaches and a fat habit of body

Did this head-packing job happen by accident or design
Part of it is "cultural" part of it "free public education"
Part hereditary dullness: Ignorance, hankering & attachment

                    "what did he say?"
Please don't disturb me. I'm busy packing
The smaller, finer bloodvessels of my brain
With peanut butter.
                What did he say. I don't know,
                But it may be useful, he said,
                Writing it in his notebook.

Sounds & perfumes twist the evening air,
If I may be allowed to mistranslate the Poet.

SRI RAMAKRISHNA: "'Is it dusk now? If it is, I won't smoke. During
the twilight hour of the dusk you should give up all other activities and
remember God.' Saying this he looked at the hairs on his arm. He
wanted to see whether he could count them. If he could not, it would
be dusk."

The pink vacuum cleaner died
Now the soul wanders the garden blue/green/black
Butterfly

there. That's for the Abyss. Now
We swing around holding onto the disgusting fur of that
Noxious body "placing our heads where our feet were"

THE SUN   THE SUN   THE SUN   (Blake shows it
Whether setting or rising
We all hang together Benjamin Franklin
Engraved bas-relief on bloody sky
Plain long and short spikes coming away from it
Statue of Liberty crown)

Isn't this extraordinary.
It only happens in the capital when I am there
Three imperial residences within walking distance
Great fat bird light through colored water
Fancy glass urns. Painted water. Break out
Around perforations. Peel coating of protective paper.
        For madness, soak in warm water to which
        a teaspoon full of ordinary baking-soda
        has been added. Twist cap on tight.

THEN SHALL BE SAID OR SUNG

        Sang-ridges! Them sang-
        ridges!
        We got to have a lot
          Of them sang-
            ridges!

And C H O C O L A T E

        "You can

        Always

          Take more,

        You know."

      Several books by Henry James

RING BELL THREE TIMES. OFFER INCENSE. RING
GONG FOR EACH OF THREE *RAIHAI*

THE RAGE OF AQUARIUS. Three kinds of
Chocolate. RUMY which is filled with raisins and
Rum syrup. . . . Chocolate strawberry cream. . . . and BLACK
Which is bittersweet
Across the street from the police-box
THE RAGE OF ANTINOUS

                        cut or tear along dotty lines
HIT GONG AGAIN. SECOND INCENSE OFFERING.
EVERYBODY CHANT.

Plum blossoms white and also red ones
Peppermint-stripe camellias, white ones resembling
Gardenia, yellow flowers of rape eaten as *sukimono*
(Rapeseed oil waterproof paper umbrella)
Tiny but   F A T   green, gold-eye bird
The light all new and different

High-test flowers cure every time
Feeling well is important and relaxes the brain
Beneficent flower vibrations continue a day or so
Now time for high-test chocolate and imaginary colors
Plum trees at Kitano Tenmangu Jinsha
Maybe I revisit tomorrow when nobody is there
I must have a secret book

Above the door to the chancel
Inside Daikakuji Zenden
Two swallow's nests, each with a little flat board
Underneath to catch the drippings
Exactly as if this were out of doors
Where kids are picnicking in the cold
All around Osawa Pond, which place
Like one or two other lakes and wells
Are only authentic remains of the Heian capital
Being fireproof and without military value
And both sides of all the wars were Japanese
Everybody liked the flowers, grass and trees
Planted around the shores. One small mudhen
Labors across the water.

At Arashiyama the flowers are late
Everybody is here anyway, walking
Under the cherry trees. They eat and play

On the river, drink *sake* and sing. The cherries
Will be obliged to bloom
No matter what weather

Man all wrapped in transparent plastic
Sloops along the wet street reciting political speech
Bullhorn slung on his shoulder
I thought first a sound truck had crawled
Onto my doorstep to die
Sun and secret perfume breeze
All greens vibrating
The dogs in the corral roaring and running
We circle them, our horses raving foam
Splash my lavender *hakama*
Green hunting-robe over yellow kimono

Lady West Gate and Lady Plum spent an hour
Quarreling over my hair, setting lacquer cap with
Horse-hair blinkers will it be a sprig of
Cherry bloom or twig of spirea
Lady Plum in tears

> (Arashiyama. Korean ladies all in blue silk
> Walking circle dance under blossoms
> Drum and gong, folksong in shoulder-slung
> Bullhorn)

I haul on the reins the horse dances to the left
Blood mixed with his foam as I fire arrows among screaming

Dogs. Lord Akiba thrown! (Heavy brocade *karaginu* and
Green *hakama* his older brother wore last year) Not a
Dog was hit the old men say:
"When we were young
all the dogs ended like sea urchins
Gently waving spikes above the sand"   Hieizan
And the Eastern Hills dark blue

                       (Old ladies with false-nose-mustaches
                       A slow comic drum dance with beerbottle
                       Spouting paper plume foam/semen)

Cherryblossom shadow
Embankment of Oi River
Young men in a circle drink and yell and sing
One performs Tanuki prick-dance with big *sake* bottle
Sometimes held out before his crotch sometimes hid
Under his shirt, Unexpected Future lurks in joybelly
He is Tanuki, magical "badger"

Wandering rusty kimono faded fag samisen
Chaunts antique lays to picnickers
Wandering showbiz drum and samisen team
Young man with family and friends & battery-driven
Electrical guitar

Sound of drum and gong prevail
But a whole school of lady *koto* players
Best kimono and Japanese hairdo

Perform on *tatami* platform underneath falling blossoms
Black hair bright silk

Elderly beerglass & bottle grandpa
Pursues green silk Korean lady
Across the pattern of the dance
She escapes and he's discomfited
Klong of gong hit with sock full of sand
Big spindle-drum hung on grandpa
Subtle GOOM.   GOOM.   Small gong tinkle-clanks,
Big gong KLONG   blue silk ladies of a certain age
The dances of Kudara
The music of Shiragi

Tanuki Badger Supernatural   RULES!
Traveler's reed hat, big *sake* jar,
Grinning mouth and blaring eyes
Grand swag belly over small upstanding prick
Huge balls hang to the ground
Spirit of mischief, wine and lechery
Long bushy tail, thick fur, nocturnal habits
"Badger" is a feeble translation . . . much more like
Big raccoon/bear
Fat breathless popeyed manifestation
Of the Divine Spirit . . . not a bad representation
Of the present writer

Japan is a civilization based upon
An inarticulate response to cherry blossoms.
So much for Western Civilization.
"Mr. Franklin, is it a setting or a rising sun?"
Try to be serious. Try to get to Toji tomorrow.
Try to remember that I accidentally found
Birthplace of Shinran Shonin when I visited Hokaiji
Magnolias and cherries at Daigoji
Unprecedented splendor.

Look into the abyss and enjoy the view.
All we see is light;   all we don't see
Is dark. We know lots of other things
With other senses. Various kinds of new green weeds
Pop up through white gravel

Chicago, Federal Court, *USA* vs *Dellinger et al.* #69 *Crim.* 180:
Mr KUNSTLER: "The whole issue in this case is language,
                    what is meant by . . ."
Mr Thomas HAYDEN, a Defendant: "We were invented."

Poetry, American. (see under *American Poetry*)
In the U.S.A. "Calliope" is a steam piano.
Nobody ever figured out that Sir Gawain's Green Knight
Was a crocodile (*pace* Yvor Winters)

Revisit Kitano plum blossoms
Pink ones have strong perfume.
Big tree in front of central sanctuary
(Gongen-Zukuri architecture, Sugawara Michizane
Was incarnation [gongen] of this Deity who presides
Over plum blossoms and calligraphy and scholarship)
So hollow and full of holes it scarcely exists at all
But blossoms immensely before scarlet fence
Intricate wooden gables
Another all propped up with poles and timbers
Part of it fixed with straw rope
Exploding white blossoms not only from twigs
And branches but from shattered trunk itself,
Old and ruined, all rotted and broken up
These plum trees function gorgeously
A few days every year
In a way nobody else does.

At the Capital
44–46 Showa
25 January

ACKNOWLEDGMENTS TO THE

GREY FOX EDITION

Thanks to The Committee on Poetry for their generous grant awarded to me in 1970.

The Gospel of Sri Ramakrishna, translated by Swami Nikhilananda, is published by the Sri Ramakrishna Math, Mylapore, Madras-4, India, 1964. All rights reserved. I am greatly indebted to the translator, Swami Nikhilananda, for his permission to quote from this great book.

Excerpt from *An Account of My Hut* (Hōjōki) by Kamo no Chōmei, translated from the Japanese by Donald Keene, from *Anthology of Japanese Literature: From the Earliest Era to the Mid-Nineteenth Century;* compiled and edited by Donald Keene. Copyright © 1955 by Grove Press, Inc.; reprinted by permission of the publisher.

Early fragments of this poem were first published in *Origin* 20, Third Series, edited by Cid Corman, Kyoto, January 1971. A version of the first eight pages was published as one of the series of Maya Quartos, edited by Jack Shoemaker and David Meltzer, printed by Clifford Burke at the Cranium Press, San Francisco, 1970. Further pages of the earlier stages of the poem appeared in *Rogue River Gorge* No. 2 (The Columbus Day Storm), edited by Michael Burgwin, Lawson Inada, and Greg Keith, at Southern Oregon College, Ashland, Oregon. *Adventures in Poetry,* edited in New York by Larry Fagin, printed yet another batch of this screed in the eighth issue. Thanks to the editors of all these publications. Seeing what some of this material would look like in print was a great help to me in cutting and revising the ms. for this present version.   P. W.

During the difficult summer of 2015, when my life was changing and my schedule was sort of wide open, I found myself taking long slow walks around my neighborhood and looking closely at flowers. One of the poems I wrote then, sitting on the bleachers by the baseball diamond in Bushrod Park, north Oakland, started: "nasturtia blossoming." If you live in northern California, you will see these orange flowers; if you read and write poetry, they may well put you in mind of Philip Whalen. They're omnipresent in his writing and drawing, and somehow talismanic. (You can also eat them, as Stephen Novotny demonstrated to me. They taste peppery. *Flowers have great medicinal virtue.*) 1966's *High-grade*, a collection of daydream doodles and calligraphic collisions, already declares "nasturtium obsession" amidst sketches of the flower. In Whalen's great bodhisattva ode to poverty and hunger, "My Songs Induce Prophetic Dreams," the poet asks:

> Beautiful turnips I peel for the soup
> Do they smell like nasturtiums
> > or chrysanthemums?

Maybe it was the nasturtiums that first put me in mind to finally go check out the Whalen archive at UC Berkeley's Bancroft Library. Laura Woltag and I had been talking about this for years (and Laura herself had been urged to check out Philip's journals by no less a poetic authority than Joanne Kyger), but I hadn't gone yet. Now that I had this space and was thinking in a renewed way about poetic vocation, composition, and form, I wondered if there might be an answer there to a question I'd been asking myself for some time: How did Philip Whalen make his miraculous booklength poem *Scenes of Life at the Capital*? Both Joanne and Alice Notley, who were kind enough to correspond with me about Philip and *Scenes of Life*, asked versions of the same question upon re-reading the text: How does it work? Joanne wrote: "I just reread *Scenes* again— amazing how he gets all those pages to hang together as one piece." And Notley wrote: "I'd say that the poem has influenced me a lot, I have tried several times for its seamless time-tracking without evident breaks in the form." It shouldn't work, but it does, as you have hopefully discovered, for the first or else the umpteenth time. (And if by chance you are one of those folks who skips to the commentary rather than reading the poem, please stop reading this right now and go read *Scenes of Life at the Capital*.)

I suspected that some kind of answer to this question, which might even be of use to me in the prosecution of my vocation of becoming an artist in a society that does not give one fuck, might be found in the notebooks and drafts from which he had composed the work.

Luckily for me the Bancroft is right down the street from where I live on Alcatraz Avenue, so with my new schedule it was no problem to go in and begin what turned out to be a years-long delve into the clothbound notebooks in which lay the raw materials of this poem (and many others). Indeed, the richness of the draft materials led me to my next question: How, from almost-daily journal writing, had Whalen shaped the materials which became the finished poem? So much lay in the journals that was absent from the final poem: How had he decided what to omit and what to include? Were there intermediate drafts between the calligraphic journal leaves ornamented with doodles and the final text Donald Allen published under the Grey Fox imprint in 1971? (The answer is yes.) What was there to learn about, not only composition, but redaction, refinement, clarification, and coordination, from this seething mass of materials?

What then do I hope? I hope here to share some of what I uncovered in the various archives I was able to visit, to unfold the material evidence of Whalen's complex process of composition, to outline some of what I have learned about form through his own experiments and meditations, and, most of all, to enrich the experience of your encounter with *Scenes of Life* and his other work and to gather a few more readers for this gentle, humble, brilliant and humane artist and teacher.

The Whalen notebooks are indeed a hidden treasure, and not only for the scholar of his poetry. The facsimiles I am able to offer here can only hint at their riches. In fact they form part of the great tradition of messy, wayward, intricate, and visionary American writing that includes Whitman's *Specimen Days* and Thoreau's *Journals*, just to stay in the nineteenth century. One of Thoreau's editors described him as "erinaceous"—that is, like a hedgehog, sticking out in all directions—and this adjective is fitly applied to Whalen's journals as well.

(This is as good a place as any to introduce beginners to Whalen's idiosyncratic practice of dating his texts. The day is written first, in Arabic numerals; the month second, in Roman numerals; and finally the last two digits of the year, again in Arabic numerals; so that 16:VI:70 is June 16, 1970 ("[Bloom's Day 64 years ago.]").)

One of the first delights of any delver into this trove is the pure pleasure of reading Whalen's calligraphic writing. Like Gary Snyder and Lew Welch (and, indirectly, Joanne Kyger), Philip learned this technique from Lloyd Reynolds, a mentor and friend at Reed College. Reynolds, who also transmitted his own love of eighteenth-century literature to Whalen, was clearly a lifelong influence on the poet, and has indirectly given us all a gift by rendering all of his handwriting luminously legible—in fact, delightful. (And oh it makes me cringe in contrast for any future reader of my dreadful handwriting!)

The visuality of the journals doesn't end with the marvelous swoops and hooks of the writing, however. Whalen's "Kyoto Journals," as I have come to call the clothbound notebooks whose contents form the raw materials for *Scenes of Life*, are also full of vibrant and colorful drawings made with felt-tip pens. As Whalen's biographer writes:

> There may be a relation between the pleasure in pure description he showed and the writing materials he used. As soon as he gets to Kyoto, he abandons the lined, pocket-size journal books, grey lead pencil, and cramped hand in favor of blank books of unfamiliar papers sewn and bound in Japanese formats. He begins to write his journal in ink with an edged pen. He discovers colored pens in the stationery stores, and these turn him on extremely. [Schneider 208]

For me, the specific question I had for the notebooks, like a suppliant to the Delphic oracle, was: What could I learn about the making of *Scenes of Life* from them? Were they, as I suspected, the raw material for the poem, and if so what was the distance between their rawness and the cooked finality of Grey Fox's 1971 publication, with Whalen in the goofy hat on the cover? You may imagine my delight when, within the first few pages of the notebook dated 15:VIII – 8:X:69, I came upon: "Loosen up. Festoon."

(Which appears in the Grey Fox edition and in this text as: *Loosten up. Festoon.*)

As I continued reading, with a copy of the published poem close to hand, I discovered that indeed much of its text was present, in some form, in the notebook before me. But not in a simple way. There were cancellations, long stretches that were omitted, reorderings, and other editorial amendments.

As Whalen complains in the poem:

To my horror & chagrin I see that I've suppressed
Lots of goody in the process of copying from ms to typewriter

L oosen up. Festoon.

An enormous drop of pure water suddenly appeared to the right of the center of the preceding page. Nothing can be done about that. ~~XXXX~~ The line was ruined. O. K.

All right.
Sure.

Really quite all right. { Gak. } All right. { Gek. }

Belt hair. A bend is funnier.
Bar Kochba. It is neither
afternoon nor evening. Try
to understand the necessity.
Do something about it like ~~that~~
animal factory mayhem in the
halls of Moctezuma. Try to
avoid regret. Why repeat. So.

Having

arrived at last and having
been carefully seated on the
floor — somebody else's floor; as

usual, — far away across the
ocean which same one looked
through Newport windows ten
years ago in somebody else's living
room ~~xxxxxxxxxxxxxxxxxxxxxxxxx~~
another messed up weedy garden
tall floppy improbable, red flowers
all the leaves turn over in the
rain to show ridged and furry
veins the hedges glisten tile roof
tin roof telephone pole decoratively
tormented black pine tree carefully
repeating endlessly regretting but
here is original done once, not
to be reproduced or electronically
remembered in whatever storage
and retrieval system.

  The Master said,

Now it is the summer of 2017, two years later, and I have dedicated the four days off in a row over the Fourth of July weekend to finally putting together something for the new edition of *Scenes* that Wave has agreed to publish (that you are holding in your hands?). Brandon and Alli went out of town and very kindly let me have use of their cottage in El Cerrito so I could spread out all my books and papers, which I can't do at home on Alcatraz Avenue because I don't have an office. In between the initial impulse to examine the Whalen materials in 2015 and now, I have read through most of the journals in the Bancroft (and taken pictures of every leaf that seemed relevant to *Scenes*), discovered a fair-copy typescript, visited the archive at Columbia and found another draft and related materials, went to Bolinas to talk to Joanne Kyger and Donald Guravich about Philip, and discussed this project with many poets including Alice Notley, Cedar Sigo, and Jason Morris. The proliferation of research and too much thought about one's materials can lead to total paralysis, like a grad student or a Thomas Bernhard character. In addition, I want to do right by Philip, who is one of the greatest American poets, a modern urban learnéd bodhisattva, and without whom I can't imagine my own work. His poems and prose works, which voyage among the diapason of rare tones from Augustan erudition and contemplative imagism through druggy detours and humble goofiness, give permission to bring forth everything in your mind as a "picture or graph of a mind moving, which is a world body being here and now which is history . . . and you." (And not to take yourself so fucking seriously while you're doing it.) In the inimitable and ultra-precise statement of poetics presented as "The Preface" to 1965's *Every Day*:

> A continuous fabric (nerve movie?) exactly as wide as these lines—"continuous" within a certain time-limit, say a few hours of total attention and pleasure: to move smoothly past the reader's eyes, across his brain: the moving sheet has shaped holes in it which trip the synapse finger-levers of reader's brain causing great sections of his nervous system—distant

galaxies hitherto unsuspected (now added to International Galactic Cat-
alog)—to LIGHT UP. Bring out new masses, maps old happy memory.

I love him, in other words. Earlier today I was crying while reading him, believe
it or not. He was polymathic without being an academic; in the words of his
'press release,' "Since You Ask Me":

> I do not put down the academy but have assumed its function in my own
> person, and in the strictest sense of the word—*academy*: a walking grove
> of trees.

Like Whitman and Williams before him, Whalen believed in the continuous
work of discovering and disseminating 'native speech.' ("'Red-ass,' they used
to say/Meaning 'home-sick,'" Whalen reports in one of several poems entitled
"Native Speech," on language heard during his time in the Army, which also
enters *Scenes*.) And like so many of our greatest authors he demonstrates a
commitment to discovering what it means, after all, to be an American, even
if the history of the nation-state that bears this name is an open-ended disaster
of which we are the inheritors. Perhaps, especially if.

Scenes of Life at the Capital is Whalen's single longest poem, and the cul-
mination of experiments in structural principles that would allow lengthier
poems to hang together. It's a text Joanne Kyger describes as "flash backs,
mutterings, trips through and outside Kyoto, personal history, world history, all
moving with the speed of thought in the moment, no bridges from here to there
in the mind, but on to the next bit of written reality." For me, it's a classic, and
part of what the study of any classic entails is what we can learn from its crafts-
manship.

(Concerning classics Whalen writes in the journals:

> the day that the study of Greek & Latin was dropped from the regular
> curriculum of gradeschool and high school studies—the day when 'edu-

cated' people could no longer read Greek or Latin with some facility (& possibly with some kind of pleasure) Western civilization came to an end, & the Modern Age commenced—Western civilization lapsed into its present degenerative cycle of war & the repression of liberty, censorship of the press & the discouragement of learning ...   )

Whalen wrote *Scenes* over the course of two sojourns in Japan, published sections of it in chapbook and magazine form while he was composing, and presented the completed work in 1971's Grey Fox edition, edited by Donald Allen. (This period is described by Whalen's biographer, David Schneider, in a chapter entitled, "Japan, Bolinas, Japan, Bolinas.") Its publication coincided with Whalen's return from Japan to Bolinas, which was very lively that year. Joe Brainard, in town for the summer, remarked on their first encounter in his *Bolinas Journal* of that year, saying that Whalen reminds him "a bit of Santa Claus. And Buddha. (Somewhere in between the two.)" And Anne Waldman recorded the invaluable long interview "Tiger Whiskers," now collected in *Off the Wall.* In response to her inquiry, "How about *Scenes of Life at the Capital,* how did you work on that?" Whalen replies:

> Oh, it was all written in notebooks while I was living in Kyoto ... Allen [Ginsberg] wrote and said that the Committee on Poetry was going to give me some money to further the cause of poetry and did I have any projects going. So I said, well, all right, I'll write this book and it'll be all about the barroom and palace life in modern and ancient Kyoto. So then the Committee on Poetry sent a lot of money, and I'm not sure, but I must've had stuff around that later got into the thing, because I had started it actually. I had started collecting the material in 1969, and it was very nice to suddenly have a whole lot of bread to take away worry and to buy lots of good food and stuff with while I was writing it, wandering up and down the town and looking at things and writing and reading. I really wanted to write a book that would be all one book in-

30 VIII 69

Wasp in the bookshelves rejects
Walt Whitman, ~~Herman~~ Melville, Emily
Dickinson, the Goliard Poets, A vedic
Reader, Lama Govinda, medieval French
verses & romances, Long Discourses of the
Buddha and the Principal Upanishads.
The window glass reads more enter=
tainingly, but soon she leaves that for
the fox tail grass the camelia hedge the
dull mid=morning sun

stead of a book broken up the way the other books are, that would just simply be all one piece, be all on one subject sort of. So simply that was in the background and I wasn't sure how it was all going to work. At one point after I'd worked on it for a year, I guess, I went into a great fit throwing out the anchor and putting on the brakes and everything because I could see there were certain ways that I got into this, but all that'll happen will be just another creepy version of *Maximus* or *Paterson*, and I didn't want to do that 'cause those things have already been done and done by experts. I didn't want to get into that act, that thing, and so I could see that the thing was not going to by any manner or means go into seven volumes, it was an important realization. So I sort of kept that in mind as I was going along but I didn't really know till I got all of the material there and started arranging it and cutting on it—I cut an immense amount out.

The time of the poem's composition is crucial to understanding its form and contents. In some ways the duration between 1969 and 1971 *is* its form. Biographical events and accidents of history form a continuous shape which is counterpointed by both personal histories and deeper collective antiquities. Additionally, publications of sections of the poem prior to the Grey Fox edition gave Whalen valuable feedback which entered into his practice. As he states in the acknowledgments to that edition, "Seeing what some of this material would look like in print was a great help to me in cutting and revising the ms. for this present version."

His notebook entry for 11:VII:70, upon receiving page proofs for the Maya Quarto chapbook of the first part of *Scenes* puts it more baldly:

It seems to make more sense now that it's all arranged into paragraphs or stanzas. Some times correcting proof is pleasant. I wonder what that book will be like when it's finished. I'm tempted to abandon it when I think it may only be a dumb imitation of *The Cantos* or *Paterson*.

The achievements of his forebears were always before him, as well as the question of how to make art that would be something other than a pale imitation—or a pretentious fraud. At the end of a lengthy evaluation of English-language authors from the eighteenth century to the present, written on 20:VI:70, he writes:

Blake & Coleridge [when they weren't having fits of Christian theological shingles] were serious artists? Can I be serious without being pompous & dull & fake?

"Can I be serious without being pompous & dull & fake?" is as good a formulation of the task of the artist as I have come across.

Like many of the life-poems which define the twentieth-century American literary landscape, *Scenes of Life* is marked by an initial compositional intention which it transcends during the time of writing, but which still leaves its mark. (In an incisive comment on Pound, whose shadow looms over this genre whether we like it or not, Robert Duncan writes "the despair of a form which Pound was suffering is actually the form of *The Cantos*.") In Whalen's case, the thematic centrality of Kyoto itself is present in the title, which recalls the souvenir photo albums of picturesque Japanese scenes manufactured for the tourist market—and, behind these, the *ukiyo-e* woodcuts of urban scenes presented in series, like those of Hiroshige's *One Hundred Famous Views of Edo*. The serial, yet discrete, images made by Hiroshige and other artists of the floating world as a response to growing urban modernity in Japan help illuminate what can seem like dizzying disjunction in Whalen's poem.

Whalen's attention to classical Japanese literature and its complex presence in modern life also runs through the poem. As Whalen puts it in "White River Ode,"

Basho and Murasaki, Seami and Buson
All used to live in this town

The first two authors make cameos in *Scenes*, as Whalen takes *shelter at Basho's Rakushisha hut*, and then, in a longer extract, visits the room advertised as the writing chamber of Lady Murasaki, "the lady who wrote *The Tale of Genji*, the greatest novel in the world" (as Whalen explains in his "Apologies, Gloss &c."):

> At the Ishiyamadera, small room with bo-leaf window
> (For the viewing of the moon, the priest explains.)
> She looks at the moon through that window that you see
> Over there. She is now a wax dummy with a face
> That exhibits what the Japanese think of as "refined"
> Features. All dressed up in Heian court robes
> Long black hair down her back. In the antechamber
> A smaller dummy represents girl-child attendant
> Grinding ink at a large inkstone
> The figure of Murasaki holds a writing brush
> And a long piece of paper. Her head has begun to turn
> Away from the writing to observe the moon
> And quite likely to remark upon the song of the uguisu
> Scholars, Japanese and Western, say she never did,
> Never was here a minute. The priest shows
> A sutra copied out in Murasaki's own handwriting
> Here's the very inkstone that she used.
> There is the moonlight window.

The notebook expands:

> It seems that Ishiyamadera was visited by Izumi-shikibu & Sei Shonagon, & by the lady who wrote the *Gossamer Diary*—not to mention any number of princes and poets—the temple was one of the favorite objects of pilgrimage during & following the Heian period. It still retains a particularly revered image of the Bodhisattva Kannon.

The venerable fake history of Murasaki draws to it the real persons of Sei Shō-nagon and other important writers of the classical period, and "any number" of poets—including Whalen. The shrine presents the complexity of attempting to seek knowledge of those *who really knew what they were doing*, who help us even across the span of centuries to figure out what the heck *we're* doing.

The diary-literature of the Heian court, contemporary with Murasaki's novel, also provides formal inspiration as in this notebook observation from 21:III:70: "The thing should stop like *The Bridge of Dreams* stops—the sensation of coming up against a beautiful stone wall <u>clonk</u>." As *Scenes* enjoins:

> *when you get to the end,*
>> *stop*

Among other things this literature demonstrates that change in customs is nothing new, as in the citation from Kamo no Chōmei's *Hōjōki* (Ten-Foot-Square Hut):

> *The manners of the capital had suddenly changed and were now exactly like those of rustic soldiers.*

Or, in the notebook on 20:V:70: "All these worlds change faster than I can finish telling you about them."

The presence of Asian classics extends to the languages themselves: Sanskrit, Chinese, Japanese, *four different texts in three incomprehensible languages*. Like many dilatory students, he scolds himself for neglecting

> *the responsibility for learning two languages (which*
> *I evade) and dim insistences of two others in the background*
> *Sanskrit and Tibetan. awk!*

Despite which the poem is in fact loaded with these languages, in forms ranging from place names and former sovereigns to foodstuffs and quotations from literary classics. Ideograms themselves make an appearance, as in the *Cantos*,

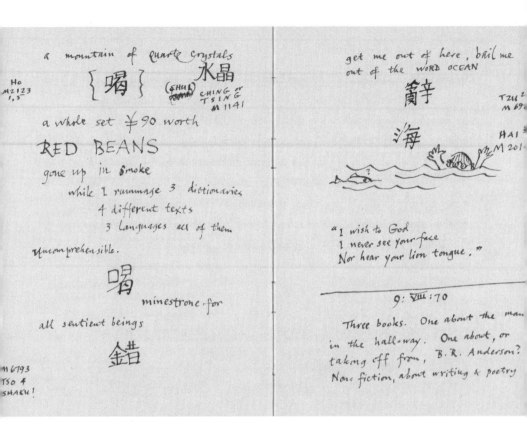

on the page in which Whalen (or his doodled self-portrait?) implores: *Bail me/ out of the WORD OCEAN!* His notebook preserves the pronunciations and the numbers of the entries in *Mathews' Chinese-English Dictionary*—perhaps for his own reference.

Just before this, Whalen calls for *minestrone for all sentient beings*—a slogan that tweaks the language of the vow taken by bodhisattvas. In Mahayana Buddhism, a bodhisattva is a being which has put off its own enlightenment in order to continue to help beings suffering in the realm of delusion. In the words of the vow, "there are numberless sentient beings; I vow to save them all." Buddhist tradition is full of famous bodhisattvas like Avalokiteshvara, who changes names and genders to become Kuan Yin in China (and later Kwannon in Japan). But the bodhisattva ideal is also an ethical standard toward which all practitioners strive.

Throughout his life Whalen had a complex relationship with religion. In an interview with Lee Bartlett, he states that he was raised "a Christian Scientist, which is theologically a very vague position," and the notebooks record [29: VI:70], "when I was an adolescent I thought it would be groovy to become an Episcopalian, like Mr. Eliot. I nearly persuaded myself to become a Catholic when I was in the Army. I discovered the Vedanta Society in Portland after the war & learned a little, but didn't join up. & now, having had lots of opportunities to study Buddhism, under marvelous teachers, I still remain 'outside.'" But the ideal was present in his work from early on, as in 1960's "A Vision of the Bodhisattvas":

"Some day you'll drop everything & become a rishi, you know."

Later on, in what I've already referred to as his bodhisattva ode, "My Songs Induce Prophetic Dreams," we read:

Transform all of this into beauty and love and the liberation of all sentient beings

where "all of this" is hunger and poverty and insufficient books and, well, the *dukkha* of life.

My own study of Whalen's work, as it connects to my life in both artistic vocation and Christian belief, has led me to the question, "What is Bodhisattva Art?"—what does it mean to make art whose aim consists in compassionate attention to all beings, with the aim that they all may be liberated? Whalen ["Heigh-Ho, Nobody's At Home"]:

When the recipient of this
wisdom is able to convey it to another human being,
to a horse, to an ant, a spider, an owl, a goldfish,

And a high cliff by words, gestures, actions

which probably affect the lives of any

such beings I'll be happy to call him a

wise man, saint, successful poet, living man, etc.

Or, in an idiom closer to the Christian scriptures, which illuminates the close ethical proximity of these traditions founded in love ["Minor Moralia"]:

"FEED THE HUNGRY. HEAL THE SICK.
RAISE THE DEAD."

there's precious little else to do

Asian literary and religious inspirations form the branches of Whalen's poem, but the roots of the shape of Scenes grow out of the whole of his prior poetic writing, an internal rhythm that must be parsed through attention to the work itself. The best way to do this yourself is to sit down with a copy of On Bear's Head and read it cover to cover. (I did this listening to a Fahey record over and over, laying on Brandon and Alli's couch in their house on Belmont, beneath the Albany Hill in El Cerrito, on the July 4th weekend of 2017 while they were out of town—somebody else's floor, as usual.) Apart from the sheer delight that is likely to ensue from such perusal, certain themes and tactics will begin to clot in your own consciousness, as part of the transmission of his own continuous nerve-movie. Lewis Freedman and I once sat in a curry house in Berkeley and discussed the way in which Whalen's compositional practice could accomplish time-travel through its practice of continuance. (This was during the same trip on which Lewis initiated a group of novice Talmudists, including myself, by means of the story wherein Moses travels in time to the classroom of Rabbi Akiba.) Early longer poems like "My Songs Induce Prophetic Dreams" are an intimation of the formal tactics that Scenes will develop and expand. By the time you've reached The Winter, you are in the outworks of Scenes—or perhaps the foothills.

Likewise, many of the poems in *Severance Pay* and *The Kindness of Strangers* draw on material related to *Scenes*, and sometimes even from the same notebooks. But by the time of the last of these collections, Philip is moving towards his monastic destiny in Zen, and the centrality of writing is beginning to recede. *Scenes* marks the high tide of his literary ambition, and his accomplishment.

In the 1971 San Francisco Poetry Center reading Whalen gave of the entirety of *Scenes of Life* (now available on PennSound, though unfortunately truncated), he begins with a brief remark about the poem and specifies that "Kyoto is not the only capital in question." It's an insight into the layering method of the poem, which is derived from Pound among other teachers, and which depends on juxtapositions and overlays whose formal similarities generate resonance, and indeed harmony. To understand how *Scenes of Life* works we must attend not only to the horizontal melody of the present-tense through-line, but also the deep historical harmonies that counterpoint the text. In addition to his deep love of eighteenth-century literature (he taught courses on Pope and other Augustan authors at Naropa), he understood his method to be informed by baroque musical practices, which are elucidated by Alice Notley in an uncollected essay:

> He always, and he meant ALWAYS, used the same underlying rhythm for his poetry: an 18th-century-type bass, almost a basso ostinato, of continuous eighth notes ... It's not that all the poetry sounds the same, or that each syllable is attached to an eighth-note, it's that underneath, there is a ghostly bass setting the pace; and Whalen does ride the same pace, even though the figuration above is various.

Notley concludes:

> The ground bass technique runs the show in ... *Scenes of Life at the Capital* ... a heroic feat of edgelessness.

(In reading notes to the poem that she shared with me, Joanne Kyger drew attention to the line "the poem runs past the edge of the page" and observes: "there is no particular beginning or end of a day, it flows . . .")

In the historical counterpoint of the poem, Kyoto, "*la cité toute proustienne*" (as Whalen writes in "The War Poem for Diane di Prima"), becomes not only the London of Doctor Johnson and the Athens of Socrates, but "Portland when I was young"—all the lost landscapes of life, somehow returning inside of this poem of exile.

To let in the plural phenomena through which we experience "all history as contemporaneous in the mind," as Pound put it, the poet's mind and body must become open to a different kind of transduction—often a sort of apparent passivity in which elements are able to combine. This reception also calls for the generation of form, indebted to the past but responsive to the present, which can make a map (or a movie) of it. In "Minor Moralia" Whalen adopts the figure of a crystal to think through how it is the world passes through our bodies:

> **For several minutes at a time I become a glowing crystal emitting rays of multicolored light. (What a metaphor . . . ugh . . . but a beginning)**

This (ugh) beginning effloresces into a reverie in *Scenes*:

> *Bottom of my waterglass, pentagonal crystal*
> *The light changes passing through, bent by glass into color*
> *and we are a rainbow, no matter how we love or hate it*

and, later, a full-on *ars poetica*:

> *Torn paper fake mountains become three-dimensional*
> *Transparent crystals. Bushes and trees all*
> *Barbered and shaved plaques of tourmaline, emerald*
> *They used to tell me I must apply myself*
> *Work hard and don't be lazy*

But what I must learn is to accomplish everything
Which has nothing to do with work.
Work is what an instrument or an engine does.
We say a crystal changes white light to green
Breaks light into rainbow, scatters it
Focuses to burning point. The crystal does
Nothing. Its shape and structure make all
The difference. Think of transistors and lasers.
In order to make this day great
Yesterday must be altered

On the theme of altering yesterday Whalen instructs the reader of his poem
for Clark Coolidge, "The Education Continues Along," to note well:

> That History, being a writing, can be destroyed, or changed to suit what-
> ever purpose the writer, the printer, the State may determine.

(A statement which correctly locates language at the center of our civil polities,
and rather ups the ante on being a poet!)

In the prose passages in the notebook from which this section is versified
and condensed, Whalen expands:

> This is what I'm doing when people come around and tell me to get busy,
> what I was doing when they used to insist on hauling me away on a point-
> less afternoon drive, Saturday or Sunday, or was doing later, when they
> insisted that I come away to a 'great' party in San Francisco. 'How can
> you be so lazy. It isn't good for you.' and 'that Philip has never done a
> day's work in his life.'

Or, as Whalen writes in "Art & Music,"

> It surprises me when I find it necessary to explain that I work every day,
> all day.

Gems, like plants, keep us company throughout *Scenes*, where we experience *the pleasure of looking at a tiny mountain of low-grade amethyst . . . crystals on top of the kitchen cabinet.* The journals remind us of medieval gem lore: "Amethyst charm against drunkenness."

But insobriety is also a visionary method, and another method of receptivity present in *Scenes* is drug use.

> *Gloomy gold morning ten* A.M. *ingest giant lump of bhang*
> *With strawberry jam from Bulgaria (friendly socialist country)*
> *Hot coffee. Things will seem better half an hour from now, OK?*

Pot, psilocybin, mescaline, alcohol—all are present, and all contribute to loading this book's rifts with ore. License for such investigation (if it were needed) was present in the adventurous drug use of his friends, including Allen Ginsberg and Jack Kerouac, and in the well-established place of intoxication in a tradition of poets including de Quincey and Coleridge. The vatic desire underpinning these experiments is voiced clearly in a poem written to his mother: "O Muse, get me high out of my mind." The journals detail elements of drug trips that don't make it into the poem, but Whalen's editing process frequently elides the beginning of drug experiences, or the end, so that the reader doesn't know the difference between headspaces, or whether the text itself is 'sober.' (Of course, the same can be said for "Kubla Khan.") As Whalen writes amidst an experience induced by a "big yellow capsule of mescaline": "Texture of this paper is quite interesting universe."

Late in the poem, Whalen puns on the familiar words of the Mass, *kyrie eleison*, with the phrase:

CURIOUS ELISION
LORD, HAVE MERCY UPON US

(As early as 1961, he was referring to the Greek of the Mass in his poem, "Statement of Condition":

that I have no real, no objective existence in the first place, much less "importance" in American literature, fame, universal admiration &c. What I really want, I guess. ✳ Contrariwise, it is embarrassing & somehow untrue when various youngsters write to tell me that I am great & that I have lots of influence on them &c. &c. Being interviewed or whatever isn't much better_ I don't enjoy it & am never satisfied by the results. Applause of a live audience, at a reading, is a temporary excitement — audience carried away by 'atmosphere' or its own enthusiasm — certainly very little effected by the poetry.

✳ There remains a tendency to think that one is in some way winning a point each time something that one has written is printed & available to lots of readers.

—✳—

17:XII:70
ANARCHY & CHAOS,
the honey pumper truck a
Day early just as I sit
down to lunch

———————

CURIOUS ELISION: LORD have mercy
upon us.

———————

20:XII:70
All of a sudden it became as if
nothing had happened and that

Kriste eleison!

Kyrie eleison!

Kriste eleison!)

Like Pound in the *Cantos*, but with many fewer pages and in a shorter span of time (and with, thank God, better politics), Whalen structures his poem according to recurring motifs, which jostle against one another to provoke new resonances as the text unfolds. In this harmonic structure, the phrase *curious elision* recurs, to remind us of what's missing, and to meditate on absence itself, the *unique abyss*, and, beneath all phenomena, the *sunyata* of Buddhist emptiness. As I began to study the drafts of the poem more closely, I realized that the poem was itself structured by 'curious elisions,' decisive omissions of draft material that shaped the resulting work in particular ways and also, perhaps, built emptiness into the poem, as a place of resonance. It works because there is an invisible hollow within it that permits it to sound, like the conch shell Whalen blows at the beginning of his 1971 reading in San Francisco—followed by the sounding of a bell.

Temple bell rings (No Self. No Permanence.)

His fascination with elision, abyss and nothing in the poem meets his love of eighteenth-century literature in a quotation from the "Wicked Earl" John Wilmot's "Upon Nothing" (stanzas 2 and 4):

Ere Time and Place were, Time and Place were not,
When primitive Nothing Something straight begot;
Then all proceeded from the great united What.

Yet Something did thy mighty power command,
And from fruitful Emptiness's hand
Snatched men, beasts, birds, fire, air, and land.

Whalen adds a little metatextual joke in his quotation:

"Then all proceeded from the great united . . ." (what?)

as though he can't remember the word that ends the line, which is in fact *what*. The Earl of Rochester meets Mahayana in ontological wordplay worthy of Beckett—in a poem that instructs, *If you want something hold out an empty hand.* (Emptiness meets in the crystal in *Juzu beads I saw today*:

each bead a white head-bone
Apparently impossible although there's enough space
Between bone crystals to drive a truck through)

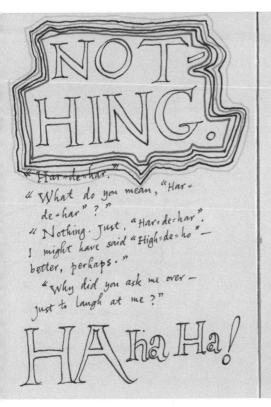

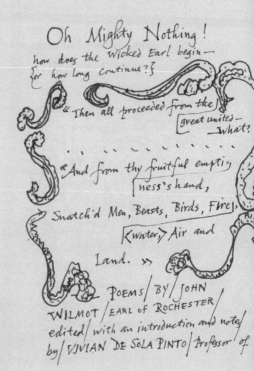

Along with *sunyata* there is *dukkha*—the Pali word the Buddha uses in the Four
Noble Truths when he teaches "existence is suffering." The Monier-Williams Dic-
tionary defines the related Sanskrit word *duhkha* as "uneasiness, pain, sorrow,
trouble, difficulty"—meanings that help us to step away from some of the tragic
grandeur "suffering" connotes, and move towards "that which is unsatisfactory,"
that maybe we wish had gone another way. *Dukkha* (or *duhkha*) is anything
that makes you go "ugh." Put like this, we can see the presence of our own at-
tachment to a particular outcome—which is relevant to a poem where almost
the first thing that happens is:

> *An enormous drop of pure water suddenly there*
> *Right in the center of preceding page*
>
> *Nothing can be done about that. The line was ruined. OK.*

The traditionally-reported last words of the Buddha are: "Decay is inherent in all compound things." Whalen's final OK is the demotic American idiom for consent to this truth, and for the discipline of practical nonattachment, which is to say continuing to behave appropriately even when things don't go the way we want them to.

This drop of water on the notebook page (which will become the first page of the printed book) sounds the theme of the elemental undoing of phenomena, and particularly the works of human artifice. This motif of destructive alteration will continue through the poem at every level of integration, as in the account of London's Great Fire of 1666:

> The Capitol's great brass dome warping
> Melting in the flames
> Hand-carved oak and myrtle and walnut paneling

A personal experience of *duhkha* takes place for Whalen in the *Shinshindo coffee house*, a frequent retreat for writing and refreshment (which is still open for business as of this writing). As Whalen writes to Diane di Prima in "The War Poem":

> I write from a coffee shop in conquered territory
> I occupy, they call me "he-na gai-jin," goofy-looking foreigner

It's here that he calamitously dowses himself with *cold sweet coffee* while reading Gerard Manley Hopkins's "To What Serves Mortal Beauty?":

> What do then? how meet beauty? Merely meet it; own,
> Home at heart, heaven's sweet gift; then leave, let that alone.
> Yea, wish that though, wish all, God's better beauty, grace.

Whatever any of that means, Whalen concludes—although it's plain from a later passage of the poem that he knows exactly what it means:

One of the most wonderful and magical actions
We can perform: Let something alone. Refuse
To allow yourself the pleasure of messing it up.

Whalen's meditation on Hopkins is also obviously a self-analysis, in which he interrogates the calm serenity of the poet-as-crystal and spills an iced coffee on it:

Poor Hopkins imagined he had it completely under control
Set framed and crystallized
It all explodes iced coffee in ten directions

Dukkha's always there, one way or another. How we respond to it is the measure of our nonattachment. Do we say, I wish this misfortune hadn't happened? Or do we put it in the poem along with everything else?

All this careful polishing and ordering of motifs forms evidence for the precise construction of a work that may appear insouciantly spontaneous at first. The effect is achieved through both a preservation of what did, in fact, happen quickly in the space of composition, and a shaping of that material through omission of what surrounds it. Understanding the movement between reception and ordering is part of trying to answer the question: How does this poem work? Witnesses to Elvis Presley's Sun session recordings, which are among his freshest and most immediate-sounding work even decades later, attest that the songs came together through dozens of takes which were themselves exploratory spaces of composition. (A friend assures me that the same phenomenon is evident in the studio sessions for the Stooges' *Raw Power*.) Whalen was thinking about folk and popular music through the entire period of composition, as evidenced by his quotations of spirituals (*I never said a murmuring word*) and, in the notebook, his citation of the lyrics of "Katie Cruel." Since the mass dissemination of recorded music began in the early twentieth century, it's come to be a privileged object for reflection on the paradox of immediacy and labor:

how can we accomplish vivid freshness through disciplined attention to the new forms that we create? Ironically enough, the very ability of writers as different as Kerouac and Frank O'Hara to evoke liveliness has often led to their dismissal as careless or even unliterary. If you think it's so easy, I invite you to try it.

Elision is, etymologically, a striking-out (from Latin *elidere*), and as the notebooks and drafts make clear, Whalen struck out extensively, and sometimes vehemently. But why 'curious'? For the same reason, I reckon, that Andrew Marvell evoked the "curious peach" in his poem "The Garden": because it is something that requires care (from Latin *cura*). In the Mahayana Buddhist tradition, the realization of *sunyata* or void is coemergent with the experience of compassion for all beings. The void calls forth care—not to sound too Heideggerian about it! As Whalen writes:

> *An awfully large number of us*
> *Had our heads bent with nowhere theories*
> *Presented in beguiling books*
> *Marx and Lenin, Freud and Jung, Churchill and Lord Keynes*
> *Kafka and Kierkegaard,*
> *In spite of or on account of which*
> *Becoming cannon-fodder for sadist politicians*

(The notebooks add: "A whole generation mentally wrecked by its concern with inferior books.")

Another motif which runs through the poem is the phrase *Fred, is that music? Do I shake or weep?* and its variations. (When I asked Diane di Prima about this poem, her first response was: "Fred, is that music?") Our educational system is no longer such that everyone will recognize this as a punning allusion to the final line of Keats's "Ode to a Nightingale": "Fled is that music:—Do I wake or sleep?" The goofiness of the pun is tempered by the dubious taste with which it alludes to the phonological cliché that native speakers of Japanese pro-

{ now all marvelously smudged
by ~~our~~ the pen of our hispid friend }
bottled somewhere near Florence
I expect that all the japanese
will rise & applaud as I leave this
                    place,
They never before having witnessed
    the consumption of wine & pizza
        by a genuine foreigner
            { i.e. white man }

Now we are a scene from life
        at the capital.
what does "SIORI" mean ?

栞

Beyond the Sanjo Bridge the
    KITAYAMA,
Northern mountains where I went
    to eat wild boar with our
resident Yalies/late in the winter
    { Social Note } 17:V, now
    Norman Holmes Pearson

is in town } I haven't been drunk
for a long time remind me of you
& your ~~dreadful~~ dreadful habit that was
10 years ago, now most of us more
sensibly take dope
        When was your last trip?
        I got high on 30 April
        Cuckoo on LSD. There's
        a great deal to be said
        for wine & I'm reading the
        faggotty part of the GREEK
        ANTHOLOGY, thinking of
        you instead of a certain youth-

Fred, is th
at music
?

nounce l-sounds as r-sounds—as in "fly shlimp," an item on the menu in "Sunday Afternoon Dinner/Fung Loy Restaurant San Francisco 25:X:62."

In the published poem the first appearance of this motif is followed by a story about "Fred," narrated by a former lover; but the poem omits notebook developments of this character including a physical description as "a large soft downy young man with big eyes and a smile six feet high or so, a student at the University his roommate a small noisy nervous kid whose dyed red hair was intended to be 'strawberry blond,'" followed by an anecdote, real or fictional I can't say, in which "Allen Ginsberg and I were hurrying through the corridors and elevators of Dwinelle Hall [at UC Berkeley], I waved at Fred as we swooped by, Allen said 'Who's that?' 'That's Fred Z.' says I. 'Hmm,' Allen said, looking back, 'he's a real good looking guy.'" "Fred Z." is written over a very thoroughly crossed out word, which may have been some person's actual name. On the next page we read:

Fred and his roommate with bottled hair
All of them yarded off to Viet Nam

There, amidst our puns and Proustian recollections, is the Vietnam War:

Events like the Indo-China War
Final quivers and tremblings
Neural flashes in freshly killed men
(movie of Bonnie & Clyde)
The longer I think about it
The more I doubt there is such a thing as
Western Civilization.

Throughout the poem we read a sometimes humorous but often scathing account of the spiritual state of America, from its foundation to the time in which Whalen was writing. Like Emily Dickinson writing during the American Civil War, the spiritual calamity of Whalen's native place engaged in the intractable Vietnam conflict entered into his writing, and it's part of the miracle of *Scenes* that it neither bogs down in despair or clots itself with jeremiads, but seeks to speak about what is dreadful as part of the weave of everything else that's already going on. In a prose reflection omitted from *Scenes* Whalen writes:

In America we are assured that individual life is infinitely valuable & must be protected, and murder must be instantly punished by death, & that the worst that can happen is death and we are afraid to die, because after death comes the judgment, heaven and hell who cannot be bribed & yet money somehow makes a magic difference, and so we kill whatever & whenever we choose, animals at the butcher store, animals in hunting season or out, any fishes, shell fishes, crustaceans, molluscs, insects, mosses, plants, rocks, mountains, rivers, our business is killing anything & everything, including people in the street, prisoners in jail, soldiers in battle.

In most of the rest of the world life is suffering, a disease, a misery, the notion of a people, a soul, a private life scarcely exists, funerals are occasions of sacrificing food and festival. A man a child might get accidentally trampled to death in a festival, but probably it's good luck to perish on a sacred occasion. Old age is an acceptable state, birds and animals not much molested, children are doted on instead of goldfish or outlandish cats & dogs, flowers are appreciated, vegetables admired as well as eaten. It is generally understood that killing people and animals brings bad luck. War between nations isn't thought of as a normal state of affairs, not a symptom of healthy government. "Live & let live" is daily acted out, seldom said.

It might be easy to dismiss this reflection as Orientalist romanticizing (or even, God forbid, the notion of a differential evaluation of life among Asian peoples that the architects of the Vietnam War promulgated in their propaganda), but I prefer to view this speculation as Whalen's attempt to take the measure of profoundly different cultures in order to bring a yardstick to bear on his own. Moreover, it is worth reflecting that this compact and lucid meditation is omitted from the poem, where instead we see its sentiment distributed throughout, in direct presentations of phenomena as well as brief snatches of rhetoric. Whalen uses what Mahayana Buddhism calls skillful means (*upaya kaushalya*) to get a message across in the way that we're able to hear it, without hectoring and objurgation. (Maybe this was another lesson he learned from the study of the *Cantos*.) In our own time, when capitalism, imperialism, militarism, and fascism have reached apocalyptic extremes, we would do well to continue in the humble study of whatever alternatives might be available to the "business [of] killing anything & everything"—and in how to best communicate those alternatives, so they can really be heard.

These are the stakes of the imagination, and as Diane di Prima memorably put it in "Rant": "The only war that matters is the war against the imagination/All other wars are subsumed in it." In his "War Poem" for Diane, Whalen touched on a similar theme, of enduring relevance:

> The war is only temporary, the revolution is
> Immediate change in vision
> Only imagination can make it work.

The National Guard murders of unarmed students at Kent State takes place during the time of *Scenes's* composition. On the day he got the news Whalen simply notes: *America is eating its children.* He memorializes the students in *Scenes* and develops the theme of relations between domestic repression, war, and economic injustice:

> *Kent State, Jackson State, There was no reason to kill them*
> *Fusillade into an unarmed crowd*
> *Of children.*
> *I can't forgive us for feeding them*
> *to the Bears currently raiding Wall Street*

As Whalen remarks in his interview with Anne Waldman, "Anyway, everything is always cross-connected."

On the theme of the political, I found one of the most striking elisions of the poem to consist in the omission of one word. In the published text, Whalen writes:

> *Almost all Americans aged 4 to 100*
> *Have the spiritual natures of Chicago policemen.*
> *Scratch an American and find a cop. There is no*
> *Generation gap.*

In the notebook, beneath a drawing of a badge with an eye labeled, "POLICE DEPT.," he specifies with more precision:

> Almost all *white* Americans, ages
> 6 to 100, have the spiritual &
> moral nature of
> New York City Irish Cops and/or
> red-neck wool-hat back-country
> sherrifs [sic] from The South.
>   I.E.
> almost any white American
> <u>is</u> a cop, whether or not
> he wears a gun and a star

I suspect the final version names "Chicago policemen" because of the trial of Bobby Seale, whose gagging in court inspired the lines:

> *Adhesive tape in Federal Court*
> *Nothing wrong with the System*
> *You'll get a chance to talk later.*
> *Federal Court held together with gum arabic*
> *And Chicago cops*

(And, on the penultimate page of the poem, the quotation from defense attorney Kunstler: "*The whole issue in this case is language. . . .*")

What stayed Whalen's hand? Why isn't the racial dynamic of the social unrest he lived through more present in the poem? An L.A. real-estate lady with *this big Marianne Moore garden party hat* says:

>   "*You don't want to*
> *live over there, Honey, there's Dark Clouds in that neighborhood.*"

among the inhabitants of the Capital
than among the folks of San Francisco —
Portland - L.A. - Seattle. ⌐ As I write
the names of these places, ~~then~~ I am aware
of no ~~longer felt~~ *suddenly overwhelming* need to ∧visit them ...
~~to~~ & doubt if I shall feel such a necessity
today.

Almost all white Americans, ages
6 to 100, have the spiritual &
moral nature of ~~an Irish Cop~~
New York City Irish Cops and/or
red=neck wool=hat back=country
sherrifs from The South.

                    I. E.

Our contemporary crisis of racialized police murder and the implication within it of all those who benefit from white supremacy ("almost any white American is a cop") makes Whalen's lost adjective feel like an essential communication.

The journals make clear that "the famous English poet" to whom Whalen keeps getting introduced is Stephen Spender, whose "most often quoted line" Whalen doesn't actually ever quote, although he paraphrases it, criticizes its euphony, and otherwise uses it as a motif through the poem *in its very absence*: "I think continually of those who were truly great." As Whalen writes:

I think all the time I can't forgive him
For jamming that "nk" sound against the initial "C"
Nor for the blackmail word, "truly"
I can't stop thinking about . . .

And, mysteriously enough, this line Whalen dislikes so much he can't bear to repeat it is, in some ways, one of the key motifs of the whole poem:

I can't stop thinking about those who really knew
What they were doing, Paul Gauguin, John Wieners, LeRoi Jones

His preoccupation with *those who really knew what they were doing* leads to repeated evaluations of nineteenth-century writers (Blake always wins), as well as to a presentation of an antecedent to Spender's verse, in Coleridge's poem "To William Wordsworth."

Or, to return to Keats's "Ode to a Nightingale":

Thou wast not born for death, immortal Bird!
No hungry generations tread thee down . . .

Or as Whalen puts it in *Scenes*, reflecting on the tragedy of Kent State:

Don't you remember being high and weeding the garden
And whatever is really beautiful can't be destroyed
We can't get our hands on it

Nyorai. Two or three star charts, one
with hour/cycle animals with buddhas
year
attached. ✳ Han shan & Shih-te,
like Chico & Harpo Marx. ✳

S.T. Coleridge : To Wm Wordsworth
ll. 50 - 57 :

... The truly great

Have all one age, & from one visible space
Shed influence! They, both in power & act,
Are permanent, & Time is not with them,
Save as it worketh for them, they in it.
Nor less a sacred Roll, than those of old,
And to be placed, as they, with gradual fame
Among the archives of mankind, thy work
Makes audible a linkèd lay of Truth,
Of Truth profound a sweet continuous lay... [77]

---

4 : IV : 70   I want to blame the
teachers of Greek language — or the Greeks them-
selves? for the intellectual "set" of the
English or Anglo-European idea of what
is poetry, what is art, what is civilization,
what is culture. Or the way — the various

These meditations do not stop with the Romantics (where Coleridge always beats Wordsworth, *poor fish*, by the way) but advance to Whalen's own generation, and in particular those whose deaths transpire in the time of the poem's composition. In the journals Whalen makes note of the death-dates of Kerouac (OBIIT JEAN-LOUIS KEROUAC/1922–1969/LOWELL, MASS.–ST. PETERSBURG, FL/21:X:69) and Charles Olson (11:I:70 OBIIT CHARLES OLSON/ at New York, aet. su. 59), but chooses to include memorials to these friends in another way. There is the abrupt notice in the middle of the poem:

> Olson dead in New York
> Jack dead in Florida.

inserted into prose written on January 25, 1970, and in orbit around them anecdotes of

> recollections of Jack in Berkeley
> Nembies & grass & wine
> Geraniums, ripe apricots, & plums

as well as an episode from 1963's Vancouver poetry conference:

> Olson sighing the while, "I hear you. One, four, three.
> I hear you. One, four, three. Minor's Ledge Light.
> One, four, three. I LOVE YOU. One, four, three, Minor's
> Ledge Light. You remember, don't you Bob. One, four, three
> I LOVE YOU—what better way to remember?"

Sometimes people act as though including the names of friends in poems is a peculiarly modern phenomenon—as though Frank O'Hara invented it. Students of the classics know that Sappho put her girlfriends' names in her poems; that Martial and Catullus were always addressing lovers and rivals; that Tu Fu wrote poems to Li Po. I'd add that the mystery and meaning of artistic friendship in our lives, especially in the midst of whatever war we inherit as well as the ongoing contempt for culture and beauty, is one of the through-lines of this poem. And poets at least since Pindar have attested that our special gift consists in attaching immortality to human names. It's one more way to think about the truly great.

Whalen was constantly thinking about, and corresponding with, his contemporaries while in Kyoto—and no one more than Joanne Kyger. A large quantity of unpublished letters attests to the vibrancy of their intellectual exchange at this time, and she makes her first appearance in *Scenes* in a lyrical passage:

> *All too soon I must leave these beauties*
> *And come away to heaven's boring towers of golden flapping*
> *Snowy wings and halo bright star crown*
> *No more to see your sexy frown and freckles*
> >   *("I can't find my mirror!*
> >   *I can't find my things!")*
> *So that when you've at last arrived there too*
> *Shall we bleak and holy strangers distant forgiving nod and smile?*
> *But soon you'll be asking me, "How do I look?*
> *Is my halo all right? I know my wings are all slaunch-wise*
> *Along the trailing edge." (Preen, preen.) "I wish I had*
> *My mirror, Kids! I wish I had all my things Oh well*
> *I don't care please hold me I want you to hang onto me a while."*

Understanding this passage turns upon the knowledge that Kyger was known to her friends as "Miss Kids" or "Kids," from her habit of greeting a room with: "Hi kids!" It's already present, longingly, in 1964's "The Best of It": "Please return daily. Look at me, Kids."

In *Scenes*, Whalen uses her familiar epithet as Lady Murasaki used titles in *Genji*, to both present and veil her characters, in a fantasized encounter in the afterlife where he ventriloquizes her desire to *hang onto me a while*.

The sense that Kyger is in some ways the occulted muse of *Scenes* deepens when we read Whalen's notebook entry for 7:V:70:

1. Why should it bother me or even interest me when Joanne decides to leave her 2nd husband & go live with a young poet.

You can only ask this question, of course, if it does bother you. In *Scenes*, this passage and feeling are redacted and versified into an episode of drinking alone:

I drink bad expensive Italian wine
Beside the Kamo River. They say
You've taken a new lover.

(The notebook adds: "[One of our friends, quite scandalized, writes that you're 10 years older.]") His journal tells us he's talking to Joanne, but the poem elides her into an anonymous second person:

I haven't been drunk for a long time
Reminds me of you, before we all
Became dope-friends.

Further on, sexual desire is acknowledged, however obliquely:

And I'm reading the faggoty part of The [Greek] Anthology
Thinking of you instead of naked boys
Curious elision.

Finally, and most revealingly:

I just realized that all I've said
For the past ten years was addressed to you
Simple and flat as that.

(The period of his friendship with Kyger had been about a decade when he wrote this line, in 1970.)

The notebook adds: "addressed to you, & that Goddess whose manifestation you are, simple & flat as that, God only knows what Clement Greenberg's going to think, Cleanth Brooks Jr., Norman Podhoretz." (Feel free to add your own updated list.)

And if this episode ended here, it might be only drunken bathos, or the melancholy of unrequited love. But the very next words are:

Kite! not the toy, a living bird
Sails above Kamogawa, that same Goddess
In worldly form dips and swings
Far below a northbound airplane
"KEE-REE!"
       "The hawk flies up to heaven"

The extremely swift and complex series of images that Whalen welds out of life in real time (including the closing citation from the Chinese *Book of Odes*, as quoted by Confucius) answers romantic despondency with a theophany, of the goddess in animal form.

Lady of Heaven
her milk for all of us
        who are the raggedy edge of everything

                                            ["Mystery Poem"]

It is one of several divine appearances throughout *Scenes* that, while often playful or satirical, also signal Whalen's profound attunement to the spiritual register of existence and his readiness to perceive signs of its presence in worldly form. Divination by birds, a globally distributed practice, is already present in 1964's "Late Afternoon":

Legge's translation, THE
DOCTRINE OF THE MEAN:

{ Chapter XII . 3. } « It
is said in the Book of Poetry,
« The hawk flies up to heaven;
the fishes leap in the deep. »

詩云，

鳶飛戾天，

魚躍于淵，

{ #239 in
Karlgren's
text }

I'm coming down from a walk to the top of Twin Peaks
A sparrowhawk balanced in a headwind suddenly dives off it:
An answer to my question of this morning

The bird's cry, *"KEE-REE!"* is certainly recorded as a rhyme with the pronounciation of *kyrie eleison*, "Lord, have mercy on us." (Whalen, transcribing the Japanese ideograms which transliterate this cry, which "(the man at the next table obligingly translates)," is so wound up that he ends up throwing his red Osmiroid pen into the river Kamo.) In the West, we may seek this mercy from Jesus; in the East, as Whalen records, "passengers remaining awake rattle their beads/ Call on Amida Buddha and Kwannon to save them." As Blake wrote, "To Mercy Pity Peace and Love/All pray in their distress." The showing forth of what Pound called "the discontinuous gods" instantiates the eternal within our sublunary world, subject to spilled coffee and great fires, to imperial wars and heartbreak:

Kite wheels above
Bridge of the Changing Moon
            that's the end of that.

(You also can't spell 'Avalokiteshvara' without 'kite,' a fact I expect Philip would not have missed.)

I didn't think I'd write about Philip and Joanne, but the poem and the notebooks have compelled me to recognize that the dynamics of their relationship are an inseparable element of the formation of *Scenes of Life*. I hope that he is now making sure her halo is all right.

Whalen's sexuality remains a mysterious and controversial topic, with claims made for his position at every place on a spectrum from pansexual to asexual, from repressed and straight to happily bi. The evidence of his poetry and notebooks suggests a definite sex drive (*Unveiling and Elevation of the Wienie*), but also a tendency to censor, tone down, or rewrite sexual content. (*Scenes* preserves his notebook observation, "I am a hunting & gathering culture," but deletes its sequel, "member of sexfiend subgroup.") The notebooks do not record

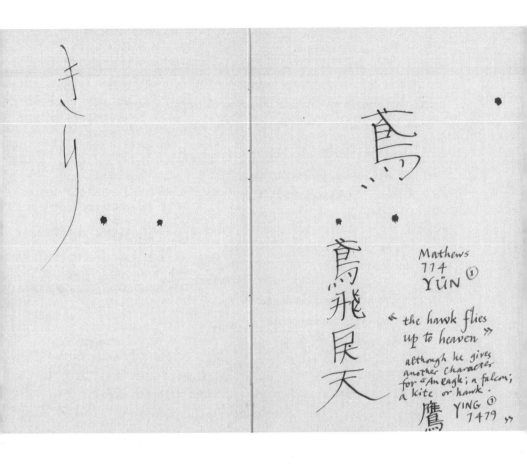

romantic or sexual partners during Whalen's time in Kyoto, though of course that doesn't mean there weren't any. It does record longing—perhaps in part because the author was writing the poem alone, in a foreign country, in his later forties, and in the midst of a spiritual wrestling that would result, before too long, in a religious vocation—like Hopkins and Donne, who both appear in Scenes.

There is more reflection on sex in the draft material for Scenes than there is in the published poem, and that's not an accident. Despite the patina of liberation and freedom around sexuality in our time, I think our discourse around its complexity is profoundly impoverished, and I don't see the prospect of insight into a sexuality as complex as Whalen's until that discourse changes.

The wayward and often wild erudition Whalen shows throughout his work can often summon up the shade of another of his heroes, Samuel Taylor Coleridge. S.T.C. is keeping Whalen company as early as 1959, when he writes in "I Am King Giant Dragon Sun":

I sit on a lime-tree branch with Coleridge
            bitching and chirping

Scenes draws *those caves of ice* from "Kubla Khan," and in the relevant notebook entry Whalen expands:

                                    Somehow or other,
S.T. Coleridge was a better poet
than any of my contemporaries
except Yeats—
        —so much for PMLA—

Whalen was enough of a Coleridgean to make his way through John Livingston Lowes's classic study, *The Road to Xanadu,* from which he quotes in "The Education Continues Along":

Give Coleridge one vivid word from an old narrative: let him mix it with two in his thought; and then (translating terms of music into terms of words) "out of these sounds he (will) frame, not a fourth sound, but a star."

Whalen's love of such lively words is present both in his published work and in the journals, where we find: "Looking again at Chaucer's *Troilus*—the word *kankedort* always catches my eye." (The lines in question come from book II, 1751–1752:

But now to yow, ye loveres that ben here,
Was Troilus nought in a kankedort

which scholar F. N. Robinson glosses, "*kankedort*, unexplained word . . ." Curious elision!)

In fact, it seems that the only writer he loves more is Blake. Perhaps it's because, as Whalen wrote in "The Greeks":

Blake tried to start all over again, good news, a new dispensation

He also continuously urges precision, since as *Jerusalem* states, "every Minute Particular is Holy." In the midst of the poem, Whalen can stop and ask himself: "Where's my minute particulars?" As though he's looking for his keys.

Of course, he is also a poet of the Capital—London—which joins Kyoto, Washington, D.C., Athens, and Rome in Whalen's meditation on empire. The cities also call to mind Freud's famous observation that Rome (one of Whalen's capitals) gives us a picture of the mind's process, with the unconscious ruins always active beneath the surface of the present.

On Valentine's Day, 1970 (also "my grandmother's birthday and the anniversary of Oregon's becoming part of the U.S.A."), beneath a drawn heart, Whalen's notebook records:

Today I received a Grant of $2500 from the Committee on Poetry, towards the composition of *Scenes of Life at the Capital*.

Shortly thereafter he reports a visit "to Maruzen to spend ¥9180 for *Blake Records*—just because I could." The extravagant purchase of G. E. Bentley's collection of contemporary biographical notices of the poet did furnish material for later sections of *Scenes*—but its acquisition was also purely for the sake of joy. Whalen was living on a very small salary, and keeping track of carfare and coffee expenditures in little notebooks you can also find in the Bancroft archive. To buy the *Blake Records* was improvident and perfectly delightful—and, after all, ended up being put "toward the composition of *Scenes of Life at the Capital*," most notably in the extract from the *Journal* of John Gabriel Stedman:

> "June 9 (1795) . . . the Apollo gardens,
> Marylebone, Madagascar bat as big as a duck . . .
> June 24 . . . How dreadful London; where a Mr. B— declared
> openly his lust for infants, his thirst for regicide,
> and believes in no God whatever.
> . . . August . . . Met 300 whores in the Strand. . . . Saw a mermaid
> (. . . September . . .) All knaves and fools and cruel to the
> excess. Blake was mobb'd and robb'd."

(Bentley notes that the *Journal* of Stedman, a retired soldier of fortune, was "an exceedingly heterodox mass of manuscripts"—Whalen appears to have drawn the second half of his quotation from Bentley, and to have drawn the first half from David Erdman's study *Blake: Prophet Against Empire*.)

I bought the *Blake Records* too, and probably excused it on account of the fact that I had to write this essay—though I love Blake too, and, like Whalen, don't really need an excuse.

In the final pages of *Scenes* we read of a ritual in honor of Tanuki, *magical* "badger," although as Whalen self-corrects later on:

> "Badger" is a feeble translation . . . much more like
> Big raccoon/bear
> Fat breathless popeyed manifestation
> Of the Divine Spirit . . . not a bad representation
> Of the present writer

Next to a notebook sketch of this Whalen reports information from Gary Snyder: "Mess around with Tanuki & you wind up drunk out of your head & 6 months pregnant." In a poem saturated throughout with ritual language and practice, from the satirized mass to the ringing of bells and *KLONG* of gongs, it makes a certain kind of shape to end with a *Tanuki prick-dance*, which brings on stage a supernatural being present among us, who however "fucks like a

Handwritten notebook facsimile:

spirit of wine and fucking
spirit of mischievous trickery
{we'd say "Coyote", we'd say
"fucks like a mink"/}
His pottery image not an unfair
~~actual as possible~~ portrait
the present writer...

//

an Interpellation:
one of my friends
always marries rich women
who expect him to find &
keep busy with an 8-hour job
Outside the house

//

AKEBI and ASHIBI is the
shrub with flowers like ~~salal~~
~~manzanita~~ [~~manz~~ Arctostaphylos]

14: IV: 70   and a long
bushy tail {"badger" is
a feeble English repre-
sentation of TANUKI —
~~the~~ "raccoon" is nearer,
& TANUKI has thick fur & noc-
turnal habits { "Mess around with TANUKI
& you wind up drunk, out
of your head & 6 months pregnant"
— G.S.S. says

15: IV: 70   As quickly as possible I
pried myself loose from the house in
order to start for the Hokaiji
16: IV: 70   & so accomplished that visit,
& one to lower Daigoji & Sanboin & the
Daigoji museum, open for cherry blossom visitors,
~~the selection of pictures has been changed since~~
new & different pictures from the one I saw
last fall. ¶ In order to get on my way, I
let one man take the first taxi that came along,
while I was waiting for the next one, a young lady
appeared near by; she wanted a taxi also, when

---

mink," as the notebook records—and is, somehow, also a picture of the author, painted in among the scenes. *Not a bad representation of the present writer.*

As the poem moves towards its conclusion we find one of its most memorable formulations:

> *Japan is a civilization based upon*
> *An inarticulate response to cherry blossoms.*

Whalen brought the memory of cherry blossoms with him, from a visit to Golden Gate Park's Japanese Tea Garden:

> That is to say, the cherry trees will blossom every year but I'll disappear for good, one of these days. There.

18 : IV : 70

~~Japan.~~ Japan is a civilization based
upon ~~the~~ an inarticulate response
to ~~these~~ cherry blossoms.

19 : IV : 70

MINATORY DREAMS

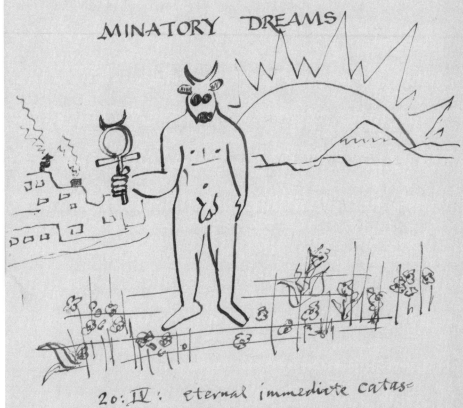

20 : IV : eternal immediate catas-
trophe.

The natural world, *slowly repeating its careful program* in a *repetition of a pattern from a long time back,* both consoles and aggravates us in our self-knowledge of mortality. In a notebook from 1971, Whalen tries out different takes on the cherry blossoms:

Cherry trees bloom.
Nothing more to do.

Cherry flowers
Nothing can be done about them

Cherry blossoms.
Look at <u>me</u>, Kids.

They need all our energy
in order to look like cherry
blossoms.

On 24:I:71 Whalen writes:

Completed revised total version [74½pp] *Scenes of Life at the Capital.* Shall I remove ALL quoted matter, make other cuts & reshuffle the continuity? Tomorrow I will think about it now is 3pm lunch time.

Just above this entry, from January 18, he records:

It is Love that rips
the veil apart like the curtains in
a Chinese restaurant
                                 whee.

In *Scenes of Life at the Capital,* Whalen followed the advice he had given years earlier, in "My Songs Induce Prophetic Dreams":

Start over. Make a continuous fabric, not a string. Try very hard.

with small variations.

_____

1: IV : 7'
Cherry trees bloom.
Nothing more to do.

_____

Cherry flowers
Nothing can be done about
    them.

_____

Cherry blossoms.
Look at <u>me</u>, Kids.

_____

They need all our energy
in order to look like cherry
    blossoms.

The poem is a continuous fabric that connects with the deep past of Japan, diverse epochs of European and American history, the present in which Whalen wrote it and my present, in which I am writing these words, as well as your, distinct, present—the time of reading. As Whalen wrote in "Historical Disquisitions": "History's now." This phenomenon of linkages is, I think, what Lewis Freedman was pointing to when he talked about Whalen as a time-traveler. We only get to this level of intricate function by trying, very hard—which is also letting oneself be in readiness, like a crystal (ugh). I have tried hard to unfold some of what I see in the 'unique abyss' of *Scenes*, but its ceaselessly generative hologram defeats any attempt I might offer at a total interpretation. That's probably on purpose. And maybe I wouldn't be doing the poem, and its author, justice, if I didn't make space for some 'curious elisions' of my own.

Whalen ends his poem where he started it, amidst *another messed-up weedy garden* on January 25, Kitano Day, when he revisits *Kitano plum blossoms* and reports in the notebook:

> One of the neighbors here in Fukuoji-cho has an old tree, all propped up with timbers & parts of it tied together with rope—full of white blossom, history, tragedy &c. &c.

Versified, this becomes the finale of a poem years in the making:

> *Exploding white blossoms not only from twigs*
> *And branches but from shattered trunk itself,*
> *Old and ruined, all rotted and broken up*
> *These plum trees function gorgeously*
> *A few days every year*
> *In a way nobody else does.*

During the difficult summer of 2015, when my life was changing and my schedule was sort of wide open, I found myself seeking clues concerning my vocation in the wild disciplined visionary notebooks of an American art bodhisattva, and seeking healing also—which came through eating the nasturtiums that were offered to me, that turned out to have a peppery taste, that had great medicinal virtue. In a way nobody else does.

Thank you Philip.

DAVID BRAZIL

INDEPENDENCE DAY – HALLOWEEN 2017

Italicized passages in this essay not otherwise cited are quotes from *Scenes of Life at the Capital*. Biographical information on Philip Whalen is now available in David Schneider's *Crowded by Beauty*. The most complete gathering of Whalen's poetry is in Michael Rothenberg's edition of *The Collected Poems*. Rothenberg also edited a festschrift volume, *Continuous Flame*, with tributes and many photographs. Informative interviews with Whalen are available in *Off The Wall*. There is almost no useful criticism on Whalen, and most of what there is reads him in the context of Beat writing and/or his friendship with Gary Snyder; see, for instance, Michael Davidson's *San Francisco Renaissance* or John Suiter's *Poets on the Peaks*. Apart from his own poetic statements and prefaces, the best writing on Whalen's practice remains that of Leslie Scalapino; see the essays collected in the new edition of *How Phenomena Appear to Unfold*.

Serious students of Whalen's work will want to visit the archive held by UC Berkeley's Bancroft Library, which includes the "Kyoto Notebooks" that form the raw material for *Scenes of Life*. Columbia University in New York and Reed College in Portland, Oregon, also have important collections of the poet's papers.

I sincerely hope this new edition of *Scenes of Life at the Capital* will draw more attention to the work of this major American writer.

ACKNOWLEDGMENTS

I owe a great debt to the many friends who have encouraged and supported me during my work on this project. Thanks to Cedar Sigo, Laura Woltag, Sara Larsen, Joshua Beckman, Kit Schluter, Lewis Freedman, Jason Morris, Stephen Novotny, Jamie Townsend, and Colter Jacobsen. Special thanks to Brandon Brown and Alli Warren for the use of their home over July 4th weekend, 2017.

Many of those who knew Philip generously shared their stories and insights with me—thanks to Joanne Kyger, Donald Guravich, Alice Notley, Diane di Prima, and David Meltzer.

I'm grateful to all the librarians, archivists, and other staff who assisted me at UC Berkeley's Bancroft Library, as well as Columbia University and Reed College. Special thanks to Dean Smith at the Bancroft.

This project would not have been possible without the support of Norman Fischer, Philip Whalen's literary executor and friend. I am grateful for his permission to print materials from Whalen's estate.

This new edition of *Scenes of Life at the Capital* is respectfully dedicated to the memory of Joanne Kyger.